The Computer: A Very Short Introduction

VERY SHORT INTRODUCTIONS are for anyone wanting a stimulating and accessible way into a new subject. They are written by experts, and have been translated into more than 45 different languages.

The series began in 1995, and now covers a wide variety of topics in every discipline. The VSI library now contains over 500 volumes—a Very Short Introduction to everything from Psychology and Philosophy of Science to American History and Relativity—and continues to grow in every subject area.

Titles in the series include the following:

AFRICAN HISTORY John Parker and Richard Rathbone
AGEING Nancy A. Pachana
AGNOSTICISM Robin Le Poidevin
AGRICULTURE Paul Brassley and Richard Soffe
ALEXANDER THE GREAT Hugh Bowden
ALGEBRA Peter M. Higgins
AMERICAN HISTORY Paul S. Boyer
AMERICAN IMMIGRATION David A. Gerber
AMERICAN LEGAL HISTORY G. Edward White
AMERICAN POLITICAL HISTORY Donald Critchlow
AMERICAN POLITICAL PARTIES AND ELECTIONS L. Sandy Maisel
AMERICAN POLITICS Richard M. Valelly
THE AMERICAN PRESIDENCY Charles O. Jones
AMERICAN SLAVERY Heather Andrea Williams
THE AMERICAN WEST Stephen Aron
AMERICAN WOMEN'S HISTORY Susan Ware
ANAESTHESIA Aidan O'Donnell
ANARCHISM Colin Ward
ANCIENT EGYPT Ian Shaw
ANCIENT GREECE Paul Cartledge
THE ANCIENT NEAR EAST Amanda H. Podany
ANCIENT PHILOSOPHY Julia Annas
ANCIENT WARFARE Harry Sidebottom
ANGLICANISM Mark Chapman
THE ANGLO-SAXON AGE John Blair
ANIMAL BEHAVIOUR Tristram D. Wyatt
ANIMAL RIGHTS David DeGrazia
ANXIETY Daniel Freeman and Jason Freeman
ARCHAEOLOGY Paul Bahn
ARISTOTLE Jonathan Barnes
ART HISTORY Dana Arnold
ART THEORY Cynthia Freeland
ASTROPHYSICS James Binney
ATHEISM Julian Baggini
THE ATMOSPHERE Paul I. Palmer
AUGUSTINE Henry Chadwick
THE AZTECS David Carrasco
BABYLONIA Trevor Bryce
BACTERIA Sebastian G. B. Amyes
BANKING John Goddard and John O. S. Wilson
BARTHES Jonathan Culler
BEAUTY Roger Scruton
THE BIBLE John Riches
BLACK HOLES Katherine Blundell
BLOOD Chris Cooper
THE BODY Chris Shilling
THE BOOK OF MORMON Terryl Givens
BORDERS Alexander C. Diener and Joshua Hagen
THE BRAIN Michael O'Shea
THE BRICS Andrew F. Cooper
BRITISH POLITICS Anthony Wright

BUDDHA Michael Carrithers
BUDDHISM Damien Keown
BUDDHIST ETHICS Damien Keown
BYZANTIUM Peter Sarris
CANCER Nicholas James
CAPITALISM James Fulcher
CATHOLICISM Gerald O'Collins
CAUSATION Stephen Mumford and Rani Lill Anjum
THE CELL Terence Allen and Graham Cowling
THE CELTS Barry Cunliffe
CHEMISTRY Peter Atkins
CHILD PSYCHOLOGY Usha Goswami
CHINESE LITERATURE Sabina Knight
CHOICE THEORY Michael Allingham
CHRISTIAN ART Beth Williamson
CHRISTIAN ETHICS D. Stephen Long
CHRISTIANITY Linda Woodhead
CIRCADIAN RHYTHMS Russell Foster and Leon Kreitzman
CITIZENSHIP Richard Bellamy
CLASSICAL MYTHOLOGY Helen Morales
CLASSICS Mary Beard and John Henderson
CLIMATE Mark Maslin
CLIMATE CHANGE Mark Maslin
COGNITIVE NEUROSCIENCE Richard Passingham
THE COLD WAR Robert McMahon
COLONIAL AMERICA Alan Taylor
COLONIAL LATIN AMERICAN LITERATURE Rolena Adorno
COMBINATORICS Robin Wilson
COMMUNISM Leslie Holmes
COMPLEXITY John H. Holland
THE COMPUTER Darrel Ince
COMPUTER SCIENCE Subrata Dasgupta
CONFUCIANISM Daniel K. Gardner
CONSCIOUSNESS Susan Blackmore
CONTEMPORARY ART Julian Stallabrass
CONTEMPORARY FICTION Robert Eaglestone
CONTINENTAL PHILOSOPHY Simon Critchley
CORAL REEFS Charles Sheppard
CORPORATE SOCIAL RESPONSIBILITY Jeremy Moon
COSMOLOGY Peter Coles
CRIMINAL JUSTICE Julian V. Roberts
CRITICAL THEORY Stephen Eric Bronner
THE CRUSADES Christopher Tyerman
CRYSTALLOGRAPHY A. M. Glazer
DADA AND SURREALISM David Hopkins
DANTE Peter Hainsworth and David Robey
DARWIN Jonathan Howard
THE DEAD SEA SCROLLS Timothy Lim
DECOLONIZATION Dane Kennedy
DEMOCRACY Bernard Crick
DEPRESSION Jan Scott and Mary Jane Tacchi
DERRIDA Simon Glendinning
DESIGN John Heskett
DEVELOPMENTAL BIOLOGY Lewis Wolpert
DIASPORA Kevin Kenny
DINOSAURS David Norman
DREAMING J. Allan Hobson
DRUGS Les Iversen
DRUIDS Barry Cunliffe
THE EARTH Martin Redfern
EARTH SYSTEM SCIENCE Tim Lenton
ECONOMICS Partha Dasgupta
EGYPTIAN MYTH Geraldine Pinch
EIGHTEENTH-CENTURY BRITAIN Paul Langford
THE ELEMENTS Philip Ball
EMOTION Dylan Evans
EMPIRE Stephen Howe
ENGLISH LITERATURE Jonathan Bate
THE ENLIGHTENMENT John Robertson
ENVIRONMENTAL ECONOMICS Stephen Smith
ENVIRONMENTAL POLITICS Andrew Dobson
EPICUREANISM Catherine Wilson
EPIDEMIOLOGY Rodolfo Saracci
ETHICS Simon Blackburn
THE ETRUSCANS Christopher Smith
EUGENICS Philippa Levine
THE EUROPEAN UNION John Pinder and Simon Usherwood
EVOLUTION Brian and Deborah Charlesworth

EXISTENTIALISM Thomas Flynn
THE EYE Michael Land
FAMILY LAW Jonathan Herring
FASCISM Kevin Passmore
FEMINISM Margaret Walters
FILM Michael Wood
FILM MUSIC Kathryn Kalinak
THE FIRST WORLD WAR Michael Howard
FOOD John Krebs
FORENSIC PSYCHOLOGY David Canter
FORENSIC SCIENCE Jim Fraser
FORESTS Jaboury Ghazoul
FOSSILS Keith Thomson
FOUCAULT Gary Gutting
FREE SPEECH Nigel Warburton
FREE WILL Thomas Pink
FREUD Anthony Storr
FUNDAMENTALISM Malise Ruthven
FUNGI Nicholas P. Money
THE FUTURE Jennifer M. Gidley
GALAXIES John Gribbin
GALILEO Stillman Drake
GAME THEORY Ken Binmore
GANDHI Bhikhu Parekh
GEOGRAPHY John Matthews and David Herbert
GEOPOLITICS Klaus Dodds
GERMAN LITERATURE Nicholas Boyle
GERMAN PHILOSOPHY Andrew Bowie
GLOBAL CATASTROPHES Bill McGuire
GLOBAL ECONOMIC HISTORY Robert C. Allen
GLOBALIZATION Manfred Steger
GOD John Bowker
GRAVITY Timothy Clifton
THE GREAT DEPRESSION AND THE NEW DEAL Eric Rauchway
HABERMAS James Gordon Finlayson
THE HEBREW BIBLE AS LITERATURE Tod Linafelt
HEGEL Peter Singer
HERODOTUS Jennifer T. Roberts
HIEROGLYPHS Penelope Wilson
HINDUISM Kim Knott
HISTORY John H. Arnold
THE HISTORY OF ASTRONOMY Michael Hoskin
THE HISTORY OF CHEMISTRY William H. Brock
THE HISTORY OF LIFE Michael Benton
THE HISTORY OF MATHEMATICS Jacqueline Stedall
THE HISTORY OF MEDICINE William Bynum
THE HISTORY OF TIME Leofranc Holford-Strevens
HIV AND AIDS Alan Whiteside
HOLLYWOOD Peter Decherney
HUMAN ANATOMY Leslie Klenerman
HUMAN EVOLUTION Bernard Wood
HUMAN RIGHTS Andrew Clapham
THE ICE AGE Jamie Woodward
IDEOLOGY Michael Freeden
INDIAN PHILOSOPHY Sue Hamilton
THE INDUSTRIAL REVOLUTION Robert C. Allen
INFECTIOUS DISEASE Marta L. Wayne and Benjamin M. Bolker
INFINITY Ian Stewart
INFORMATION Luciano Floridi
INNOVATION Mark Dodgson and David Gann
INTELLIGENCE Ian J. Deary
INTERNATIONAL MIGRATION Khalid Koser
INTERNATIONAL RELATIONS Paul Wilkinson
IRAN Ali M. Ansari
ISLAM Malise Ruthven
ISLAMIC HISTORY Adam Silverstein
ISOTOPES Rob Ellam
ITALIAN LITERATURE Peter Hainsworth and David Robey
JESUS Richard Bauckham
JOURNALISM Ian Hargreaves
JUDAISM Norman Solomon
JUNG Anthony Stevens
KABBALAH Joseph Dan
KANT Roger Scruton
KNOWLEDGE Jennifer Nagel
THE KORAN Michael Cook
LATE ANTIQUITY Gillian Clark
LAW Raymond Wacks
THE LAWS OF THERMODYNAMICS Peter Atkins
LEADERSHIP Keith Grint
LEARNING Mark Haselgrove

LEIBNIZ Maria Rosa Antognazza
LIBERALISM Michael Freeden
LIGHT Ian Walmsley
LINGUISTICS Peter Matthews
LITERARY THEORY Jonathan Culler
LOCKE John Dunn
LOGIC Graham Priest
MACHIAVELLI Quentin Skinner
MAGIC Owen Davies
MAGNA CARTA Nicholas Vincent
MAGNETISM Stephen Blundell
MARINE BIOLOGY Philip V. Mladenov
MARTIN LUTHER Scott H. Hendrix
MARTYRDOM Jolyon Mitchell
MARX Peter Singer
MATERIALS Christopher Hall
MATHEMATICS Timothy Gowers
THE MEANING OF LIFE Terry Eagleton
MEASUREMENT David Hand
MEDICAL ETHICS Tony Hope
MEDIEVAL BRITAIN John Gillingham and Ralph A. Griffiths
MEDIEVAL LITERATURE Elaine Treharne
MEDIEVAL PHILOSOPHY John Marenbon
MEMORY Jonathan K. Foster
METAPHYSICS Stephen Mumford
MICROBIOLOGY Nicholas P. Money
MICROECONOMICS Avinash Dixit
MICROSCOPY Terence Allen
THE MIDDLE AGES Miri Rubin
MILITARY JUSTICE Eugene R. Fidell
MINERALS David Vaughan
MODERN ART David Cottington
MODERN CHINA Rana Mitter
MODERN FRANCE Vanessa R. Schwartz
MODERN IRELAND Senia Pašeta
MODERN ITALY Anna Cento Bull
MODERN JAPAN Christopher Goto-Jones
MODERNISM Christopher Butler
MOLECULAR BIOLOGY Aysha Divan and Janice A. Royds
MOLECULES Philip Ball
MOONS David A. Rothery
MOUNTAINS Martin F. Price
MUHAMMAD Jonathan A. C. Brown
MUSIC Nicholas Cook
MYTH Robert A. Segal
THE NAPOLEONIC WARS Mike Rapport
NELSON MANDELA Elleke Boehmer
NEOLIBERALISM Manfred Steger and Ravi Roy
NEWTON Robert Iliffe
NIETZSCHE Michael Tanner
NINETEENTH-CENTURY BRITAIN Christopher Harvie and H. C. G. Matthew
NORTH AMERICAN INDIANS Theda Perdue and Michael D. Green
NORTHERN IRELAND Marc Mulholland
NOTHING Frank Close
NUCLEAR PHYSICS Frank Close
NUMBERS Peter M. Higgins
NUTRITION David A. Bender
THE OLD TESTAMENT Michael D. Coogan
ORGANIC CHEMISTRY Graham Patrick
THE PALESTINIAN-ISRAELI CONFLICT Martin Bunton
PANDEMICS Christian W. McMillen
PARTICLE PHYSICS Frank Close
THE PERIODIC TABLE Eric R. Scerri
PHILOSOPHY Edward Craig
PHILOSOPHY IN THE ISLAMIC WORLD Peter Adamson
PHILOSOPHY OF LAW Raymond Wacks
PHILOSOPHY OF SCIENCE Samir Okasha
PHOTOGRAPHY Steve Edwards
PHYSICAL CHEMISTRY Peter Atkins
PILGRIMAGE Ian Reader
PLAGUE Paul Slack
PLANETS David A. Rothery
PLANTS Timothy Walker
PLATE TECTONICS Peter Molnar
PLATO Julia Annas
POLITICAL PHILOSOPHY David Miller
POLITICS Kenneth Minogue
POPULISM Cas Mudde and Cristóbal Rovira Kaltwasser
POSTCOLONIALISM Robert Young

POSTMODERNISM Christopher Butler
POSTSTRUCTURALISM Catherine Belsey
PREHISTORY Chris Gosden
PRESOCRATIC PHILOSOPHY Catherine Osborne
PRIVACY Raymond Wacks
PSYCHIATRY Tom Burns
PSYCHOLOGY Gillian Butler and Freda McManus
PSYCHOTHERAPY Tom Burns and Eva Burns-Lundgren
PUBLIC ADMINISTRATION Stella Z. Theodoulou and Ravi K. Roy
PUBLIC HEALTH Virginia Berridge
QUANTUM THEORY John Polkinghorne
RACISM Ali Rattansi
REALITY Jan Westerhoff
THE REFORMATION Peter Marshall
RELATIVITY Russell Stannard
RELIGION IN AMERICA Timothy Beal
THE RENAISSANCE Jerry Brotton
RENAISSANCE ART Geraldine A. Johnson
REVOLUTIONS Jack A. Goldstone
RHETORIC Richard Toye
RISK Baruch Fischhoff and John Kadvany
RITUAL Barry Stephenson
RIVERS Nick Middleton
ROBOTICS Alan Winfield
ROMAN BRITAIN Peter Salway
THE ROMAN EMPIRE Christopher Kelly
THE ROMAN REPUBLIC David M. Gwynn
RUSSIAN HISTORY Geoffrey Hosking
RUSSIAN LITERATURE Catriona Kelly
THE RUSSIAN REVOLUTION S. A. Smith
SAVANNAS Peter A. Furley
SCHIZOPHRENIA Chris Frith and Eve Johnstone
SCIENCE AND RELIGION Thomas Dixon
THE SCIENTIFIC REVOLUTION Lawrence M. Principe
SCOTLAND Rab Houston
SEXUALITY Véronique Mottier
SHAKESPEARE'S COMEDIES Bart van Es
SIKHISM Eleanor Nesbitt
SLEEP Steven W. Lockley and Russell G. Foster
SOCIAL AND CULTURAL ANTHROPOLOGY John Monaghan and Peter Just
SOCIAL PSYCHOLOGY Richard J. Crisp
SOCIAL WORK Sally Holland and Jonathan Scourfield
SOCIALISM Michael Newman
SOCIOLOGY Steve Bruce
SOCRATES C. C. W. Taylor
SOUND Mike Goldsmith
THE SOVIET UNION Stephen Lovell
THE SPANISH CIVIL WAR Helen Graham
SPANISH LITERATURE Jo Labanyi
SPORT Mike Cronin
STARS Andrew King
STATISTICS David J. Hand
STUART BRITAIN John Morrill
SYMMETRY Ian Stewart
TAXATION Stephen Smith
TELESCOPES Geoff Cottrell
TERRORISM Charles Townshend
THEOLOGY David F. Ford
TIBETAN BUDDHISM Matthew T. Kapstein
THE TROJAN WAR Eric H. Cline
THE TUDORS John Guy
TWENTIETH-CENTURY BRITAIN Kenneth O. Morgan
THE UNITED NATIONS Jussi M. Hanhimäki
THE U.S. CONGRESS Donald A. Ritchie
THE U.S. SUPREME COURT Linda Greenhouse
THE VIKINGS Julian Richards
VIRUSES Dorothy H. Crawford
VOLTAIRE Nicholas Cronk
WAR AND TECHNOLOGY Alex Roland
WATER John Finney
WILLIAM SHAKESPEARE Stanley Wells
WITCHCRAFT Malcolm Gaskill
THE WORLD TRADE ORGANIZATION Amrita Narlikar
WORLD WAR II Gerhard L. Weinberg

Darrel Ince

THE COMPUTER

A Very Short Introduction

OXFORD
UNIVERSITY PRESS

Great Clarendon Street, Oxford OX2 6DP

Oxford University Press is a department of the University of Oxford. It furthers the University's objective of excellence in research, scholarship, and education by publishing worldwide in

Oxford New York

Auckland Cape Town Dar es Salaam Hong Kong Karachi Kuala Lumpur Madrid Melbourne Mexico City Nairobi New Delhi Shanghai Taipei Toronto

With offices in

Argentina Austria Brazil Chile Czech Republic France Greece Guatemala Hungary Italy Japan Poland Portugal Singapore South Korea Switzerland Thailand Turkey Ukraine Vietnam

Oxford is a registered trade mark of Oxford University Press in the UK and in certain other countries

Published in the United States by Oxford University Press Inc., New York

First published 2011

British Library Cataloguing in Publication Data
Data available

Library of Congress Cataloging in Publication Data
Data available

Typeset by SPI Publisher Services, Pondicherry, India
Printed and bound by
CPI Group (UK) Ltd, Croydon, CR0 4YY

ISBN: 978-0-19-958659-2

Contents

List of illustrations

Chapter 1
The naked computer

Introduction

One of the major characteristics of the computer is its ability to store data. It does this by representing a character or a number by a pattern of zeros and ones. Each collection of eight zeros and ones is known as a 'byte'; each individual one or zero is known as a 'bit' (binary digit). Computer scientists use various terms to describe the memory in a computer. The most common are the kilobyte, the megabyte, and the gigabyte. A kilobyte is 10^3 bytes, a megabyte is 10^6 bytes, and a gigabyte is 10^9 bytes.

The first computer I used was an Elliot 803. In 1969, I took a computer-programming course at my university which used this computer. It was situated in a room which was about 40 foot by 40 foot, with the hardware of the computer contained in a number of metal cabinets, each of which would fill almost all of the en-suite bathroom I have at home. You submitted your programs written neatly on special paper to two punch tape operators, who then prepared a paper-tape version of the program. Each row of the paper tape contained a series of punched dots that represented the individual characters of the program.

The program was then taken to the computer room, the tape read by a special-purpose piece of hardware, and the results displayed on a device known as a Post Office Teletype; this was effectively a typewriter that could be controlled by the computer, and it produced results on paper that were barely of better quality than toilet paper.

The storage capacity of computers is measured in bytes; the Elliot computer had 128 thousand bytes of storage. It used two cabinets for its memory, with data being held on small metallic rings. Data were fed to the computer using paper tape, and results were obtained either via paper or via a punch which produced paper tape. It required an operator to look after it, and featured a loudspeaker which the operator could adjust in volume to check whether the computer was working properly. It had no connection to the outside world (the Internet had yet to be invented), and there was no hard disk for large-scale storage. The original price of the first wave of Elliot 803s was £29,000, equivalent to over a hundred thousand pounds today.

While I am writing this chapter, I am listening to some Mozart on a portable music device known as an MP3 player. It cost me around £180. It comfortably fits in my shirt pocket and has 16 gigabytes of memory – a huge increase over the capacity of the only computer at my old university.

I typed this book on a computer that was known as a netbook. This was a cut-down version of a laptop computer that was configured for word processing, spreadsheet work, developing slide-based presentations, and surfing the Internet. It was about 10 inches by 6 inches. It also had 16 gigabytes of file-based memory used for storing items such as word-processed documents, a connection to the Internet which downloaded web pages almost instantaneously, and a gigabyte of memory that was used to store temporary data.

There is clearly a massive difference between the Elliot 803 and the computers I use today: the amount of temporary memory, the amount of file-based memory, the processing speed, the physical size, the communications facilities, and the price. This increase is a testament to the skills and ingenuity of the hardware engineers who have developed silicon-based circuits that have become smaller and more powerful each year.

This growth in power of modern computers is embodied in a law known as 'Moore's law'. This was expounded by Gordon Moore, the founder of the hardware company Intel, in 1965. It states that the density of silicon circuits used to implement a computer's hardware (and hence the power of a computer) will double every eighteen months. Up until the time of writing, this 'law' has held.

The computer has evolved from the physical behemoths of the 1950s and 1960s to a technological entity that can be stored in your jacket pocket; it has evolved from an electronic device that was originally envisaged as something only large companies would use in order to help them with their payroll and stock control, to the point where it has become an item of consumer electronics as well as a vital technological tool in commercial and industrial computing. The average house will contain as many as 30 computers, not only carrying out activities such as constructing word-processed documents and spreadsheet tables, but also operating ovens, controlling media devices such as televisions, and regulating the temperature of the rooms.

Even after 70 years, the computer still surprises us. It surprised a number of computer scientists in the fifties, who predicted that the world only needed a small number of computers. It has surprised me: about 20 years ago, I saw the computer as a convenient way of reading research documents and sending email, not as something that, combined with the Internet, has created a global community that communicates using video technology, shares photographs, shares video clips, comments on news, and reviews books and films.

Computer hardware

One aim of this book is to describe how the computer has affected the world we live in. In order to do this, I will describe the technologies involved and the applications that have emerged over the last ten years – concentrating on the applications.

First, the basic architecture of the computer; I will describe this architecture in a little more detail in Chapter 2. This is shown in Figure 1. The schematic shown in this figure describes both the earliest computers and the newest: the basic architecture of the computer has not changed at all over 60 years.

At the heart of every computer is one or more hardware units known as processors. A processor controls what the computer does. For example, it will process what you type in on your computer's keyboard, display results on its screen, fetch web pages from the Internet, and carry out calculations such as adding two numbers together. It does this by 'executing' a computer program that details what the computer should do, for example reading a word-processed document, changing some text, and storing it into a file.

Also shown in Figure 1 is storage. Data and programs are stored in two storage areas. The first is known as main memory and has the property that whatever is stored there can be retrieved very quickly. Main memory is used for transient data – for example, the result of a calculation which is an intermediate result in a much bigger calculation – and is also used to store computer programs while they are being executed. Data in main memory is transient – it will disappear when the computer is switched off.

Hard disk memory, also known as file storage or backing storage, contains data that are required over a period of time. Typical entities that are stored in this memory include files of numerical data, word-processed documents, and spreadsheet tables. Computer programs are also stored here while they are not being executed.

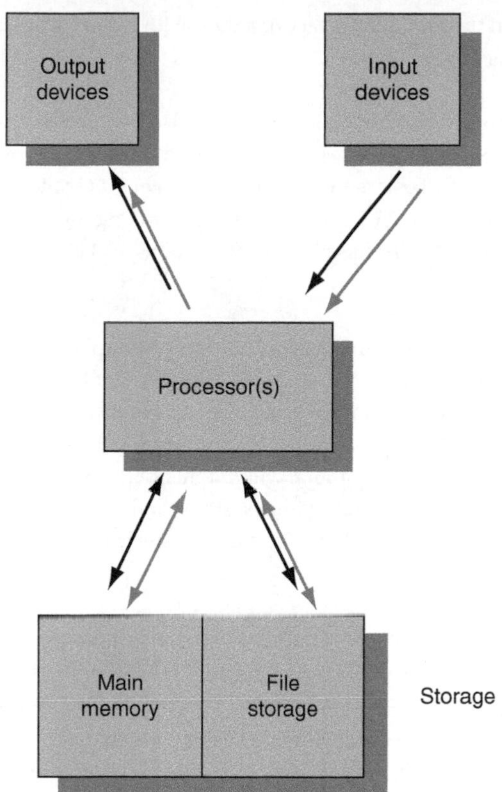

1. The architecture of a computer

There are a number of differences between main memory and hard disk memory. The first is the retrieval time. With main memory, an item of data can be retrieved by the processor in fractions of microseconds. With file-based memory, the retrieval time is much greater: of the order of milliseconds. The reason for this is that main memory is silicon-based and all that is required to read data there is for it to be sent along an electronic circuit. As you will see later, hard disk memory is usually mechanical and is stored on the metallic surface of a disk, with a mechanical arm retrieving the data.

Another difference between the two types of memory is that main memory is more expensive than file-based memory; consequently, there is usually far less main memory in a computer than file-based memory (I have a laptop that has 3 gigabytes of main memory and the file-based memory contains 500 gigabytes of storage).

Another set of components of a computer are input devices. These convey to the computer what the user requires of the programs executed by the computer. The two devices that you will have met most frequently are the keyboard and the mouse. There are, however, a number of other devices: touch screens that you find on iPods and satellite navigation systems and pressure monitors found as part of the instrumentation of a nuclear power station are two further examples.

The final component of a computer is one or more hardware devices that are used to display results. There are a variety of such devices. The most familiar to you will be the computer monitor and the laser printer; however, it can also include advertising displays found at events such as football matches, the console that displays flight data on the instrumentation found in the cockpit of a plane, the mini-printer that is used to produce a supermarket receipt, and the screen of a satellite navigation device.

The working definition of a computer that I shall use within this book is:

> A computer contains one or more processors which operate on data. The processor(s) are connected to data storage. The intentions of a human operator are conveyed to the computer via a number of

> input devices. The result of any computation carried out by the processor(s) will be shown on a number of display devices.

You may think this statement is both pedantic and self-evident; however, I hope that you may see as this book unfolds that it has a number of radical interpretations.

Before leaving this section, it is worth looking at another indicator of the growth in power of computers. In their excellent book *The Spy in the Coffee Machine*, O'Hara and Shadbolt describe the progress made in computer-based chess. To be good at chess requires you to look ahead a number of moves and evaluate what your opponent would do for each of these moves, and then determine what move you would make for each of these moves, and so on. Good chess players hold lots of data in their heads and are able to carry out fast evaluations. Because of this, the computer has always been seen as potentially a good chess player.

The chess programs that have been written effectively store lots of moves and countermoves and evaluate them very quickly. O'Hara and Shadbolt describe how in 1951 a computer could only think ahead two moves, in 1956 a computer could play a very restricted game of chess on a smaller board but would take upward of 12 minutes to make a move. However, in 1997 a computer beat the world champion Gary Kasparov. This progress is partly due to improvements in software techniques for game playing; the major reason though is that computers have become faster and faster.

The Internet

Computers do not operate in isolation: most are connected to a computer network. For most computers, this will be the huge collection of computers and communication facilities known as the Internet; however, it could be a network that controls or monitors some process, for example a network of computers that keep a plane flying, or a network of computers used to monitor the traffic flow into and out of a city.

The Internet has had a major effect on the way computers are currently being used; so it will be worthwhile looking briefly at how it interacts with a typical computer – say the PC that you use at home.

The Internet is a network of computers – strictly, it is a network that joins up a number of networks. It carries out a number of functions. First, it transfers data from one computer to another computer; to do this, it decides on the route that the data takes: there is a myth that when you carry out some activity using the Internet, for example downloading a web page, the connection between the computer holding the page and your computer is direct. What actually happens is that the Internet figures out a route that the data takes via a number of intermediate computers and then routes it through them. So when you see a web page displayed on your computer, that page may have been split into blocks of data, with each block having travelled through a number of continents and traversed a number of intermediate computers belonging to companies, universities, charitable organizations, and government organizations.

The second function of the Internet is to enforce reliability. That is, to ensure that when errors occur then some form of recovery process happens; for example, if an intermediate computer fails then the software of the Internet will discover this and resend any malfunctioning data via other computers.

A major component of the Internet is the World Wide Web; indeed, the term 'Internet' is often used synonymously with the term 'World Wide Web'. The web – as I shall refer to it from now on – uses the data-transmission facilities of the Internet in a specific way: to store and distribute web pages. The web consists of a number of computers known as *web servers* and a very large number of computers known as *clients* (your home PC is a client). Web servers are usually computers that are more powerful than the PCs that are normally found in homes or those used as office computers. They will be maintained by some enterprise and will contain individual web pages relevant to that enterprise; for example, an online book store such as Amazon will maintain web pages for each item it sells.

The program that allows users to access the web is known as a *browser*. When you double-click the browser icon on your desktop, it will send a message to the web asking for your home page: this is the first page that you will see. A part of the Internet known as the Domain Name System (usually referred to as DNS) will figure out where the page is held and route the request to the web server holding the page. The web server will then send the page back to your browser which will then display it on your computer.

Whenever you want another page you would normally click on a link displayed on that page and the process is repeated. Conceptually, what happens is simple. However, it hides a huge amount of detail involving the web discovering where pages are stored, the pages being located, their being sent, the browser reading the pages and interpreting how they should be displayed, and eventually the browser displaying the pages.

I have hidden some detail in my description. For example, I have not described how other web resources such as video clips and sound files are processed. In a later chapter, I will provide a little more detail. At this point, it is just worth saying that the way that these resources are transferred over the web is not that different to the way that web pages are transferred.

The Internet is one of the major reasons why computers have been transformed from data-processing machines to a universal machine that can, for example, edit music files, predict the weather, monitor the vital signs of a patient, and display stunning works of art. However, without one particular hardware advance the Internet would be a shadow of itself: this is broadband. This technology has provided communication speeds that we could not have dreamed of 15 years ago. Most users of the Internet had to rely on what was known as a dial-up facility which transferred data at around 56 kilobits of data a second. When you consider that the average web page size is around 400 kilobits, this means it would take around 7 seconds for a web page to be displayed in your browser. In the 1990s, companies used dedicated communications hardware to overcome this lack of speed.

Unfortunately, the average user was unable to do this until broadband became generally available.

Typical broadband speeds range from one megabit per second to 24 megabits per second, the lower rate being about 20 times faster than dial-up rates. As you will see later in the book, this has transformed the role of the home-based computer.

Software and programs

The glue that binds all the hardware elements shown in Figure 1 together is the computer program. When you use a word processor, for example, you are executing a computer program that senses what you type in, displays it on some screen, and stores it in file-based memory when you quit the word processor. So, what is a computer program?

A computer program is rather like a recipe. If you look at a recipe in a cookbook, you will see a list of ingredients and a series of instructions that will ask you to add an ingredient, mix a set of ingredients together, and place a collection of ingredients in an oven. A computer program is very much like this: it instructs the computer to move data, carry out arithmetic operations such as adding a collection of numbers together and transfer data from one computer to another (usually using the Internet). There are, however, two very important differences between recipes and computer programs.

The first difference is size. While a typical recipe might contain about 20 lines of text, computer programs will contains hundreds, thousands, or even millions of lines of instructions. The other difference is that even a small error can lead to the catastrophic failure of a program. In a recipe, adding four eggs instead of three may result in a meal with a slightly odd taste or texture; however, mistyping the digit 1 instead of 2 in a million-line program may well result in a major error – even preventing the program running.

There are a variety of programming languages. They are categorized into high-level and low-level languages. A high-level language, such as Java or C#, has instructions that are translated to many hundreds of the individual instructions of the computer. A low-level language often has a one-to-one relationship with the basic computer instructions and is normally used to implement highly efficient programs that need to respond to events such as the temperature of a chemical reactor becoming critical.

Every few days the media features a story about a software project that has overrun or is over budget or a computer system that has dramatically failed. Very rarely can these failures be attributed to a failure of hardware. The failures occur for two reasons. The first reason for a malfunctioning of an existing computer system is technical error, for example a programming error that was not detected by testing. The second reason is due to managerial failings: projects that overrun or dramatically exceed their budgets tend to occur because of human factors, for example a poor estimate of project resources being produced or a customer changing their mind about the functions a system should implement.

My own view is that given the complexity of modern computer systems, it is hardly surprising that projects will be late and that errors will be committed by developers.

Book themes

The first theme of the book is how hardware advances have enabled the computer to be deployed in areas which would have been unheard of a decade ago. The circuit that a computer processor is deposited on can be easily held in the palm of one hand rather than in a large metal cupboard. A memory stick containing 16 gigabytes of data can easily be attached to a key-ring. Moore's law implies that the computational power of a computer processor doubles every two years. You can now buy hard disk storage of 500 gigabytes for under £60. There are a number of implications. The first is that in the past decade computers have been able to do things few people dreamt of in the 1990s, for example British Telecom's Vision programme that brings television over the Internet. The second is that the reduction in size of computer hardware has enabled them to be physically deployed in environments which would have been impossible a few years ago.

The second theme is how *software* developers have taken advantage of advances in hardware to produce novel applications. An example of this is that of MP3 players such as the Apple iPod. The iPod, and other devices such as the Sony Walkman, obviously rely on advances in hardware. However, they also rely on a software-based technique which, when applied to a sound file, compresses it so that it occupies 10% of its original size without an appreciable decline in sound quality.

A third theme is how the Internet has enabled computers to be connected together in such a way that they behave as if they were just one big computer. This is embodied in an idea known as 'cloud computing' whereby data, rather than being stored in a local database, are held in a number of computers connected to the Internet and may be accessed by programs that can be developed by Internet users who have relatively low-level programming skills.

Allied to this idea is that of the Internet as a huge resource of data which the computer user can tap into. This includes data such as that published by the British government's data.gov.uk and US government's Data.gov programs, but also data that have been contributed directly or indirectly by users of the Internet. For example, there are sites that enable you to home in to your town or village and examine the broadband speeds that are being experienced by your neighbours, the data that these sites contain having been donated by the users of the site.

A fourth theme is how the Internet has provided creative facilities that were only available to professionals. For example, computer hardware advances, software advances, and advances in the technologies used to create video cameras mean that anyone can become a film director and display their results on the Internet. A computer user can now buy hardware and software for less than a thousand dollars that enables them to reproduce the features of a recording studio of the 1990s.

A fifth theme is how advances in computer processor hardware have enabled number-crunching applications which, until a few years ago, were regarded as outside the realm of computation. Moore's law implies that computer processors become twice as powerful as they were eighteen months previously. The consequence of this is that over the past decade, processors have become many times more powerful and, combined with other hardware improvements such as the increased speed of data-storage devices means that, for example, simulations involving the natural world – for example, simulations of hurricanes – can now be easily carried out without deploying powerful supercomputers.

A sixth theme is how the computer has become a disruptive technology in that it has both transformed and eliminated many skills. An example here is photography. When I visit a tourist site, I hardly ever see film cameras being used: almost invariably, small palm-sized digital cameras are now the norm. Moreover, the photographs that are taken can be brought home in a memory stick, placed in a home computer, and then printed. Relatively cheap programs such as Adobe Photoshop can now be used to improve these photographs by, for example, adjusting the exposure.

No longer does the development of a photograph involve the dousing of a film in chemical baths in a darkroom. This is clearly an improvement; however, there is another side to the coin which has resulted in fewer job opportunities for photographers. There is a web site known as Flickr. This is a photo-sharing site where Internet users upload photographs and display them to visitors to the site. Newspaper editors who want cheap stock photographs for an issue of their paper (for example, a picture of a robin for a Christmas edition) can purchase such a picture for a fraction of the amount that they would have to pay a freelance photographer.

A seventh theme is that of the insecure computer. A computer that stands alone with no connections to a network is perfectly safe from any technological attack; the only threat that the owner of the computer should be aware of is that of having it stolen. However, very few computers are in this state: most are connected to the Internet. This means that they become prone to a large variety of attacks, from those that create a mild nuisance effect to serious attacks which can completely stop a computer from working. An example of this is the zombie computer. This is a computer attached to the Internet that has been compromised by a hacker, a computer virus, or a Trojan horse.

The most common use for a zombie computer is to act as a mail server and send spam email; this is email that tries to sell you something you don't need (Viagra, cheap stocks and shares, or pornographic publications, for example) or attempts to steal information such as your bank account identity. Most owners of such computers are unaware that their system is being used in this way. It is because the owner tends to be unaware that they are referred to as 'zombies'. In May 2009, the security company McAfee estimated that there were around 12 million new zombies attached to the Internet. This is really quite an extraordinary figure for a computer infestation.

Some examples

Before looking at these themes in more depth, it is worth examining some examples of the themes in action.

The Norwegian oil company StatOil uses blue mussels to monitor any leaks around their oil rigs. When there is an oil leak, the mussels contract their shells. Concerned with the environmental and revenue impacts of leaks during oil drilling, StatOil sought a way to replace a manual process that involved submersible vehicles and included deep-sea divers. What they did was to attach RFID tags to the shells of blue mussels. These are small, silicon-based, data-holding chips that also include a computer. When the blue mussels sense an oil leak, they close; this makes the RFID tags emit signals that indicate this event has occurred; these signals are picked up by a computer on the rig which then shuts down the activity that was causing the leak. For example, if drilling were taking place, the drilling line would be automatically stopped. This unusual application is possible as a consequence of advances in the miniaturization of computer circuits.

Google Inc. is the company that hosts the hugely popular search engine known as Google. One of the things that the search engine does is to store the queries made by the users so, for example, you can visit a Google web site and discover which are the most popular queries. In 2008, the fastest-rising queries from the

United Kingdom were: 'iPlayer', 'facebook', 'iphone', 'youtube', 'yahoo mail', 'large hadron collider', 'Obama', and 'friv'. Most of these terms are associated with hugely popular web sites or electronic devices such as the iPhone. The last entry, 'friv', is an online games site.

As you will see later, a huge amount of information can be obtained from the queries that users submit to a search engine. It is now common practice for police investigators to explore the use of a search engine by a suspected murderer. In a murder where the victim's neck was broken, they would check for search terms such as 'neck', 'snap', 'break', 'rigor mortis', and 'body decomposition' which the murderer might have submitted to the search engine.

An interesting application of the massive amount of stored data that Google keeps of the queries that are made is in tracking influenza. Two Google engineers tracked the incidence of queries such as 'thermometer', 'flu symptoms', 'muscle aches', and 'chest congestion', and compared the location of the Internet users who made the queries against the US Center for Disease Control database and discovered a very close correlation: in effect, they discovered that the volume of queries involving the search words was similar to the density of flu cases. You can now access a web site managed by Google Inc. that shows the growth of flu cases in a number of countries over a period of time.

This is an example of a major theme of this book: that of the computer not only having access to the data on its own hard drive, but also to the massive amount of data stored on the computers spread around the Internet.

Another example of a use of computers beyond the limited visions of the 1970s and 1980s concerns the way that computers are connected together in order to work collaboratively.

Researchers in the applied sciences have for the past 20 years tried to squeeze processing power from their computers. For example, the Human Genome Project has mapped the gene structure of humankind and researchers are now using this information to detect the genetic causes for many types of illness. This work has required the use of expensive supercomputers that contain a large number of processors. However, a number of researchers in this area, and in other areas such as climatology, have come up with the novel idea of asking the public to run processor-intensive programs.

A good example of this is Folding@home. This project looks at the structure of proteins in order to detect therapeutic regimes that can be used for treating patients with conditions such as Alzheimer's disease. Researchers involved in this project have enlisted around 30,000 home computers to spread the computational load. Volunteers use their spare processor and memory capacity to take a small part of a computer program that carries out protein simulation and produce results that are fed back to a master computer that coordinates the processing.

This is not the only application of a technique known as 'mass computing' or 'mass collaboration'. There are projects that attempt to analyse the radio waves from outer space in order to discover whether there is intelligent life beyond our universe, those that simulate atomic and sub-atomic processes, and many projects associated with molecular biology. In the past, supercomputers containing a large number of processors situated in a small number of research institutes were used – and indeed are still used – however, hardware advances and the increasing availability of the broadband Internet has meant that we can all participate in major research projects with little effect on our home computers.

wordia is a visual dictionary that anyone can access via their home computer. It contains words of course, but each word is accompanied by a video of someone telling you what the word means to them. It is one of the most delightful web sites that I have come across and is an example of the phenomenon known as mass collaboration in action. This is an example of an application related to a major theme of the book: that of the computer being part of a loosely coupled global computer.

Another example involves the construction of computer circuits. As engineers try to squeeze more and more electronic components onto silicon chips, the design of such chips becomes much more difficult: for example, placing two metallic connections close to each other would cause electrical interference that would result in the circuit malfunctioning. Given that millions of such circuits might be manufactured and embedded in computers, a mistake would be hugely expensive for the manufacturer. The complexity of design is such that the only viable way to develop the architecture of a silicon-based circuit is by using the computer itself.

The programs that are used to design computer circuits try to optimize some design parameter; for example, one class of programs attempts to squeeze connections on a silicon chip in such a way that the maximum number of connections are deposited subject to a number of constraints: that connections are not too close to each other and that the heat dissipation of the circuit does not rise past some threshold which would affect the reliability of the circuit. There are a number of techniques used for optimization; one recent very efficient class of programs is based on animal and insect behaviour.

An example of this is a technique known as 'swarm optimization' in which a number of computer processes collaborate with each other in order to discover an optimal solution to a problem using the simple mathematics used to describe how shoals of fish or flocks of birds behave. Here is an example of another theme of this book: the ingenuity of the programmer combined with hugely increased speeds that enable complex tasks to be carried out that even a small number of years ago would have been impossible to even think about.

Swarm optimization is an example of the revolution in the use of computers that has happened over the past two decades: it is represented by the progression of the computer that just carries out mundane processing steps such as calculating a wage bill to applications such as designing computers and controlling the inherently unstable fighter planes that have become the norm in our armed services.

So far, I have concentrated on computers and their uses that are visible. There are many, many more applications where the computer is not seen. My nearest city is Milton Keynes. When I drive to the city and then around its severely practical road system, I pass many, many unseen applications of the computer. I pass a speed camera controlled by a small microprocessor; a company that fabricates electronic equipment using robots controlled by a computer; the street lighting controlled by a very small, primitive computer; the Milton Keynes Hospital where most of the monitoring equipment that is used could not function without an embedded computer; and the shopping centre, where computers are used to keep the environment within each shop strictly controlled.

Increasingly, computers are being used in hidden applications where failure – either hardware or software failure – could be catastrophic and, indeed, has been catastrophic. For example, the Therac-25 was a computer-based radiation therapy machine which had a number of software problems. In the late 1980s, a number of patients received massive overdoses of radiation because of problems with the computer interface.

An example of a hidden application where failure can be catastrophic and which is an example of another theme is that of the control of an oil rig. A functioning oil rig draws extremely flammable oil or gas out of the earth, burns some of it off and extracts unusable by-products such as hydrogen sulphide gas from the oil. In ocean-based installations, this required a large number of human operators. Increasingly, however, computers are being used to carry out tasks such as controlling the flow of oil or gas, checking that there is no spillage, and regulating the burn-off process.

There have been instances of IT staff hacking into the software systems that are, for example, used to monitor oil rig operations, either for financial gain or because they had become disgruntled. What is not realized is that although computer crime such as spreading viruses is still prevalent there are whole collections of applications of computers that are just as vulnerable to attack. The SINTEF Group, a Norwegian think tank, has reported that offshore oil rigs are highly vulnerable to hacking as they move to less labour-intensive, computer-controlled operations – for example, the wireless links that are used to remotely monitor the operation of a rig and to keep a rig in its position via satellite navigation technology are particularly vulnerable.

This book

Each of the chapters of this book is centred about a theme that I have outlined in this chapter.

'The Small Computer' will describe how a computer architecture is mapped to silicon and the problems that the computer designer has to face when pushing more and more electronic components onto a piece of silicon. Topics that will be discussed here and in other chapters include: very large-scale integration, silicon fabrication, the hardware design process, and new techniques and technologies for design such as the use of artificial intelligence programs to maximize or minimize some factor such as heat dissipation.

'The Ubiquitous Computer' will describe how miniaturization has led to the computer becoming embedded into a variety of electronic and mechanical devices. Examples discussed in this chapter and other chapters: RFID tags, the use of supermarket loyalty cards, computers used for the monitoring of the infirm or elderly, wearable computers, computers used within virtual reality systems, and the convergence that is occurring between the phone, the MP3 player (iPod), and the computer.

'The Global Computer' will look at how the Internet has enabled large numbers of computers to be connected together in such a way that they can be used to attack wicked problems – that is, problems that are computationally very difficult to solve. The chapter starts by looking at one particular computationally wicked application from genome sequencing. I will then describe a concept known as grid computing where very large numbers of computers are connected together in such a way that their spare capacity can be used to attack such hard problems. The chapter will conclude by looking ahead to the seventh chapter and briefly describe how the grid concept has become commercialized into something known as cloud computing. This involves regarding the Internet as just one huge computer with almost infinite computing power and data-storage facilities.

'The Insecure Computer' looks at some of the threats – both technological and human – that can result in major security problems. The chapter will cover the whole panorama of attacks including virus attacks, Trojan attacks, denial of service attacks, spoofing attacks, and those that are caused by human error. The chapter will look at the defences that can be employed, including firewalls, intrusion detectors, virus checkers, and the use of security standards. A strong point that I make is that technological defence is not enough but that it has to be melded with conventional security controls.

'The Disruptive Computer' describes how the computer has had a major disruptive effect. Most of the examples describe disruption engendered by the combination of the computer and the communications technologies employed in the Internet. It will examine how in media industries, for example newspapers, have declined over the last five years and how online advertising has eaten into the revenues of television companies. The concluding part of the chapter will examine a number of areas where computers have de-skilled, transformed, moved, or eliminated certain jobs.

'The Cloud Computer' describes how the Internet has enabled not just developers but moderately skilled individuals to treat this network like a massive computer. A number of companies such as Amazon provide public access to huge product databases and programming facilities in such a way that applications can be developed that mesh across a number of areas. This has led to the concept of the cloud computer: huge numbers of processors and databases connected by the Internet with software interfaces that anyone can use. The chapter introduces the idea of software mashing: the process whereby sophisticated applications can be constructed by integrating or 'mashing' large chunks of existing software.

'The Next Computer' is a relatively short chapter. It looks at some of the blue-skies work that is being carried out by researchers in an attempt to overcome the limitations of silicon. It will focus on quantum computing and biological computing. A quantum computer is a computer that carries out its processes using quantum effects such as entanglement to operate on data. It is very early days as yet, but theoretical studies and some early experiments have indicated that huge processing speed-ups are possible with quantum computers.

The effect of such computers could be devastating. For example, much of commercial computing depends on cryptographic techniques that rely on the huge computational complexity of certain classic number processing algorithms. Quantum computers may be capable of making these algorithms solvable and hence open up the Internet to easy attack.

The chapter will also describe the principles behind the DNA computer. This is a half-way house between current computer technology and quantum computers. DNA computers use the genetic properties of biological strands to provide very large parallel processing facilities. Effectively, DNA computers implement a large number of hardware processors which cooperate with each other to solve hard computational problems.

A major idea I hope to convey to you in Chapters 4 and 7 is that regarding the computer as just the box that sits on your desk, or as a chunk of silicon that is embedded within some device such as a microwave, is only a partial view. The Internet – or rather broadband access to the Internet – has created a gigantic computer that has unlimited access to both computer power and storage to the point where even applications that we all thought would never migrate from the personal computer are doing just that.

An example of this is the migration of office functions such as word processing and spreadsheet processing – the bread and butter of many home computers. Google Inc. has launched a set of office tools known as Google Apps. These tools are similar to those found in Microsoft Office: a word processor, a spreadsheet processor, and presentation package similar to PowerPoint etc.

Chapter 2
The small computer

Introduction

The last 30 years has seen an amazing improvement in the capability of computers in terms of their processing speed, size of memory, cost, and physical size. Processors have increased their power from around 90 kIPS in the early 1970s to many thousands of MIPS in the second decade of the 21st century. The speed of a processor is expressed in instructions per second (IPS) where an instruction is some action that the computer takes, for example adding two numbers together; the prefix 'k' stands for a thousand, while the prefix 'M' stands for a million.

Memory capacity has also increased: the Elliot 803 computer that I described in the previous chapter contained 128 k bytes of memory held in a cabinet the size of a dozen coffins: my iPod contains 16 gigabytes of storage.

How has this increase in speed and memory capacity happened? In this chapter, I answer this question; however, before doing so, it is worth looking briefly at how data and computer programs are held in the computer.

The binary number system

We are all used to the decimal system of numbering. When you see a number such as 69126, what it stands for is the number

$$6\times10^4+9\times10^3+1\times10^2+2\times10^1+6\times10^0$$

where each digit represents the result of multiplying itself by a power of ten (any number raised to the power 1, for example 10^1, is always itself, in this case 10, and any number raised to the power zero is always 1).

We say that the base of a decimal number is 10; this means that we can express any decimal number using a digit between 0 and 9. With binary numbers, the base is 2; this means that we can interpret a binary number such as 11011 as

$$1\times2^4+1\times2^3+0\times2^2+1\times2^1+1\times2^0$$

and it will have the decimal value 27 (16+8+0+2+1).

Numbers are stored in binary form in this way. Text is also stored in this form as each character of the text has an internal numeric equivalent. For example, the American Standard Code for Information Interchange (ASCII) is a standard used throughout computing to designate characters. The code assigns a numeric value for each character that can be stored or processed by a computer – for example, the capital A character is represented by a binary pattern equivalent to the decimal number 65.

The binary system is also used to represent programs.
For example, the pattern

1001001110110110

might represent an instruction to add two numbers together and place them in some memory location.

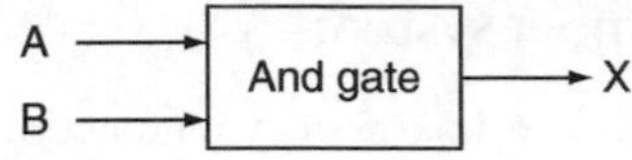

2. A schematic of an And gate

Computer hardware

A computer will consist of a number of electronic circuits. The most important is the processor: this carries out the instructions that are contained in a computer program. As you will remember from the preceding chapter, there are two types of memory: main memory used to store relatively small quantities of data and file-based memory which is used to store huge amounts of data such as word-processor files.

There will also be a number of other electronic circuits in a computer: for example, if you look at the back of a desktop computer, you will often see a black rod attached to a metal strip. The rod contains the aerial that picks up wireless signals from a device known as a modem that connects to the Internet. Behind the strip will be a circuit that converts the signals that are picked up by the aerial into a form that can be used by the computer so that, for example, it can display a web page on your monitor.

There are a number of individual circuit elements that make up the computer. Thousands of these elements are combined together to construct the computer processor and other circuits. One basic element is known as an And gate, shown as Figure 2. This is an electrical circuit that has two binary inputs *A* and *B* and a single binary output *X*. The output will be one if both the inputs are one and zero otherwise. This is shown in a tabular form known as a truth table; the truth table for the And gate shown in Figure 2 is shown in Table 1.

Table 1. The actions of an And gate

A	B	X
0	0	0
0	1	0
1	0	0
1	1	1

There are a number of different circuits inside the computer – the And gate is only one example – when some action is required, for example adding two numbers together, they interact with each other to carry out that action. In the case of addition, the two binary numbers are processed bit by bit to carry out the addition.

So, how does a computer do its work? The best way to describe this is to outline what happens when I use a word processor. When I click the MS Word icon on my desktop, the Windows operating system senses the click and then loads the MS Word word processor into the main memory of the computer.

The program then starts executing. Each time I carry out some action the word-processor program senses it and part of its program code is executed. The execution is carried out in what is known as the fetch-execute cycle. Here the processor fetches each programming instruction and does what the instruction tells it to do. For example, an instruction may tell the computer to store what I have typed in a file, it may insert some text into some part of the word processed document, or it may quit the word processor.

Whatever actions are taken by a program such as a word processor, the cycle is the same; an instruction is read into the processor, the processor decodes the instruction, acts on it, and then brings in the next instruction.

So, at the heart of a computer is a series of circuits and storage elements that fetch and execute instructions and store data and programs. Over the last 70 years, a variety of technologies have been used for constructing a computer. The very first computers were based on electrical relays; these were mechanical switches which would have two states: binary one would be represented by the relay being closed, while zero would be represented by a relay being open. When you hear a computer programmer talking about a 'bug' in their program, the term comes from the use of relay computers. In 1946, Grace Hopper, one of the pioneers of computer programming, joined the Computation Laboratory at Harvard University where she worked on early relay computers. She described how they traced a program error to a moth trapped in a relay, coining the term 'bug' for a software error.

The first real generation of computers used electronic circuits based around devices known as valves. These looked a bit like small light bulbs and could be switched electronically from a zero (off) to a one (on) state via a signal to the valve. Programmers communicated with these computers using paper tape or punched cards which either held data to be processed or the programs that carried out the processing.

The main memory that was used in early computers employed circular pieces of magnetic material known as cores. These stored binary one or binary zero depending on their magnetized state.

First-generation computers were succeeded by second-generation computers that used transistors. A transistor was a lump of silicon that could be switched on and off; the Elliot computer I described in the previous chapter relied on such a technology.

During the late 1960s and early 1970s, physicists, materials scientists, and electronic engineers managed to deposit the circuits that were implemented by transistors in second-generation computers onto silicon chips. This is a process known as Very Large Scale Integration (VLSI). These third-generation computers are the ones we use today. It is VLSI that has been the technology that has provided the incredible miniaturization, speed, and capacity of today's computers. Miniaturization, exemplified by the width between components, has decreased from around 1.00 μm in the early 1990s to 40 nm in the early part of the 21st century. The symbol μm stands for a millionth of a metre, and the symbol nm stands for a nanometre – one thousandth of one millionth of a metre.

Computer circuits

Modern computer hardware relies on silicon. There are a number of manufacturing steps that are carried out to transform a block of silicon into a processor or an interface circuit such as the one used to drive the monitor of a computer.

The first step is the growing of a single crystal of silicon as a cylinder. When the growth of the cylinder has been completed, circular slices known as 'wafers' are cut from the cylinder in the same way that you would cut slices from a cylinder of luncheon meat, the only difference being that the slices are usually a fair bit thinner than the meat. After the slices have been cut, they are polished.

The next step is to embed a design on each silicon wafer for the circuit that is to be implemented. This is done via a device known as a photo-mask. This is a grid that lays out the pattern of the circuit on the wafer together with the components of the circuit. Ultraviolet light is shone through the grid onto a portion of the wafer and this forms the guidelines for the circuit to be deposited on it. Normally a number of similar circuit plans are etched onto the silicon wafer.

In detail, the fabrication process proceeds as follows. First, the silicon wafer is baked in an oven filled with oxygen. This forms a thin layer of silicon dioxide on the surface. The wafer is then coated with another thin layer of an organic material known as a resist. So we now have a silicon base, often known as a substrate, a silicon dioxide layer, and a resist layer at the top.

Ultraviolet light is then shone through the mask onto a portion of the wafer. The structure of the resist is broken up by the light but the remaining layers are unaffected. The process is very similar to the way that a black and white photograph is developed. Once a portion of the wafer has had the light shone on it the mask is moved and the next part of the wafer has the pattern etched.

The next stage is for the wafer to be fabricated. This involves placing it along with many other wafers in a bath of solvent which dissolves those parts of the resist that have received the ultraviolet light.

The silicon wafer will now have a layer of silicon, a layer of silicon dioxide, and the part of the resist layer that has been unaffected by the ultraviolet light. The part of the wafer that has been removed by the solvent will have exposed areas of silicon dioxide. These are then removed by applying another solvent which will expose the underlying silicon.

The silicon wafer will now contain a layer of silicon parts which are exposed, a silicon dioxide layer which will have sections cut out of it exposing the silicon, and the resist which will have the same sections cut as the silicon dioxide.

The next step is to remove the resist by using a solvent that dissolves it. The wafer now contains a base layer of silicon with the circuit pattern etched in it. The exposed part of the silicon layer is then treated in order to make it capable of conducting electrical signals. The wafer now has treated silicon which represents the circuit and new silicon dioxide that acts as an insulator which ensures that signals that pass though one part of the silicon do not affect other signal paths.

Further layers are then deposited to complete the circuit with the last layer being one of silicon dioxide. This is etched with holes that enable connections to be made with the underlying circuits.

The process of packaging the circuits now starts. There are a variety of packaging techniques. I shall describe the simplest. First, square metallic connections known as pads are deposited around the edge of each circuit. Another layer of silicon dioxide is then placed on the wafer with holes etched in the layer to enable connections to be made to the pads.

Each circuit is then tested by a special purpose piece of electronic equipment which will engage with the pads and send signals to some of the pads and monitor the effect of the signals on other pads. Any circuit that fails the test is marked with a dye and eventually rejected. If the circuits pass the test, another layer of silicon dioxide or silicon nitride is placed over the circuit and connection holes made in the layer to the pads. This final layer acts as physical protection.

The final step is to cut each circuit from the silicon wafer. This is achieved by a mechanical cutter; this is similar in concept to the way that a glazier will cut a shape out of glass. The wafer has now become a collection of identical chips.

The final step is for each chip to be mounted in some sort of frame in order that it can be fitted into a computer. There are a variety of techniques for this. A simple one involves attaching the chip on a lead frame using an adhesive that helps conduct heat away from the chip and then placing signal wires on the chip that connect with the pads. Once the wires are added, the chip is covered in some plastic-based material as a final protection.

If you are interested in more details, the excellent book *BeBOP to the Boolean Boogie: An Unconventional Guide to Electronics* by Clive Maxfield is a great introduction to computer electronics (see Further reading).

Computer memory

There are two sorts of memory devices: read-only memory (ROM) devices and read-write memory (RWM) devices. The former hold data that cannot be altered; the latter can be erased and data rewritten.

Computer memory is implemented as silicon and is fabricated in the same way that hardware processors and other circuits are fabricated. The only difference between a computer memory and, say, the circuit that communicates with the Internet or the processor is that the former has a regular structure.

Figure 3 shows the typical layout of memory. It consists of an array of cells that are implemented as transistors. Each cell can hold either a zero or a one. Each horizontal collection of cells is known as a word and the depth of the array is, not unsurprisingly, known as the depth.

A circuit known as an address bus is connected to the array. Each word in the array has a unique identity known as its address. When data from memory or a program instruction are required by the processor of the computer, a signal is sent along the bus; this instructs the memory unit to decode the address and make the data or program instruction available at the specified location available to the processor.

There are a variety of memory devices available. Mask-programmed ROMs have their data or programs placed in them when they are fabricated and cannot be changed. Programmable Read Only Memories, commonly known as PROMs, are fabricated

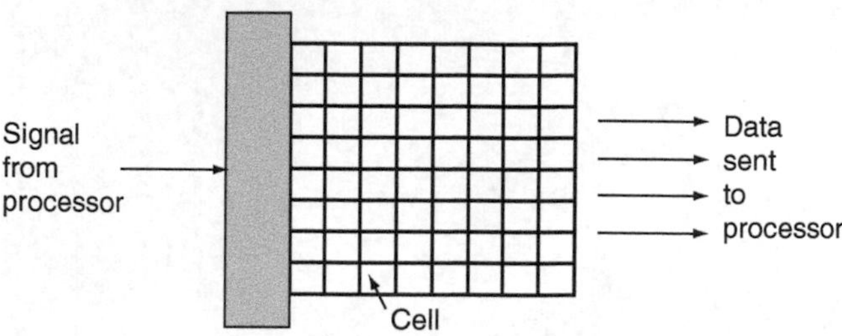

3. Computer memory

in such a way that they are blank and can then be programmed using an electronic device. However, since they are read-only this can only happen once – they cannot be reprogrammed.

Erasable Programmable Read-Only Memory, more commonly known as EPROM, goes one step further than PROMs in that it can be erased and then reprogrammed. There is confusion about EPROMs: since they can be reprogrammed, there is the impression that their contents can be changed by overwriting when they are in the computer. Overwriting can only be achieved by a special-purpose piece of equipment in which the EPROM device is inserted.

A major step forward that bridged the worlds of read-only memory and writable memory was the development of Electrically Erasable Programmable Read Only Memory, often known as EEPROM. This is a form of EPROM that can be erased while it forms part of a computer. A technology known as flash memory has been developed using the ideas and technologies associated with EEPROM.

Flash technology is employed in applications where a large amount of non-erasable memory is required. For example, it is used in the USB memory sticks that are used to transfer data from one computer to another, or as backup storage in case a computer

4. A hard disk unit

fails. Other applications that use flash technology include personal digital assistants, laptop computers, digital audio players, digital cameras, and mobile phones. A new-generation small laptop computer known as a netbook employs flash memory for the storage of programs and files of data.

Writable memory is implemented using a number of technologies. Dynamic Random Access Memory (DRAM) is the most common memory used within computers. It is implemented in such a way that it can potentially lose its data over a short period of time. Because of this, the contents of DRAM cells are read and written to continually in order to recharge its data.

Static Random Access Memory (SRAM) is a technology that does not require refreshing to be applied to its cells unless a program alters the cell or the power is removed from the computer it is contained in. It is faster but more expensive than DRAM.

File-storage technology

The technologies that I have described so far are normally used for relatively small amounts of data (it is a remarkable consequence of the advances in miniaturization and fabrication that I can refer to 8 Gb as 'relatively small'). For larger quantities of data and programs, a different, much slower technology is employed. It is known as hard disk technology.

In essence, a hard disk unit consists of one or more circular metallic disks which can be magnetized. Each disk has a very large number of magnetizable areas which can either represent zero or one depending on the magnetization. The disks are rotated at speed. The unit also contains an arm or a number of arms that can move laterally and which can sense the magnetic patterns on the disk. The inside of a hard disk unit is shown in Figure 4; here, the arm is clearly visible close to the edge of the disk.

When a processor requires some data that is stored on a hard disk, say a word processor file, then it issues an instruction to find the file. The operating system – the software that controls the computer – will know where the file starts and ends and will send a message to the hard disk to read the data. The arm will move laterally until it is over the start position of the file and when the revolving disk passes under the arm the magnetic pattern that represents the data held in the file is read by it.

Accessing data on a hard disk is a mechanical process and usually takes a small number of milliseconds to carry out. Compared with the electronic speeds of the computer itself – normally measured in fractions of a microsecond – this is incredibly slow.

Because disk access is slow, systems designers try to minimize the amount of access required to files. One technique that has been particularly effective is known as caching. It is, for example, used in web servers. Such servers store pages that are sent to browsers for display. If you look at the pattern of access to the web pages associated with a web site, you will find that some pages are retrieved very frequently – for example the home page – and some pages accessed very little. Caching involves placing the frequently accessed pages in some fast storage medium such as flash memory and keeping the remainder on a hard disk.

Another way of overcoming the slow access times to hard disks is to replace them completely with electronic storage media such as flash memory. Currently, such technologies do not approach the storage capacity and cost of hard disk units: typically flash memory can be bought up to 64 Gbytes and for the same price you can buy a hard disk of 500 Gbytes. However, for some types of computer which have modest storage requirements electronic memory for the bulk storage of files is now feasible. For example, some computers feature electronic storage media bulk storage rather than a hard disk. Such computers contain low power processors and the use of this memory compensates for this.

Future technologies

The last 30 years have seen amazing progress in miniaturization. There are, however, some performance and size plateaus which will be reached comparatively soon. For example, as you pack more and more components onto a silicon chip, they become more error-prone due to random signals being generated; another problem is that a phenomenon known as sub-atomic erosion kicks in, destroying the structures in the silicon. There are also design problems that occur with highly miniaturized circuits.

In the final chapter, I shall look at two radical ideas that will, if successful, transform computing. These are the use of biological materials for circuits and the deployment of quantum physics ideas in the development of processors; these require very long-term research. There are, however, other low-level technologies and materials that are currently being researched and developed for computer circuits. They include the use of optical lithography to produce components that are faster, the use of optical connections between components, the replacement of silicon by carbon, and the use of superconducting materials for the circuits within a computer.

Chapter 3
The ubiquitous computer

Four examples of ingenuity

A couple of years ago, I parked my car early in Milton Keynes, and as I was waiting to use the automatic ticketing machine, I noticed that the previous customer was a parking attendant. I made some remark about the expenses of his job being rather heavy if he has to park in Milton Keynes and whether he got an employee discount; he told me that his reason for getting a parking ticket was not to stick it on the windscreen of his car but as evidence that he had started work at the designated time – he was effectively using the machine as a time clock.

In *The Spy in the Coffee Machine*, Nigel Shadbolt and Kieron O'Hara describe an innovative use of the computer in Japan. The Japanese have a major problem with age drift: the birth rate of the country is one of the lowest in the world and immigration is discouraged. As a consequence, the population of Japan is rapidly ageing and there is an increased need to look after the elderly. One way that this is being achieved is via computer-based devices. One of these is the iPot. This is a kettle that keeps coffee or soup warm all day. Whenever the iPot is used a message is sent to a server and, twice a day, a report on the frequency of use is sent to a relative or carer either by a mobile phone text message or via email to satisfy them that those who are looked after are in good health.

The Japanese company NEC has developed a new type of spectacle that can project messages onto the retina of a user. There are a number of uses for such a device: two examples are to help staff who use computers in call centres and to provide a running translation when a conversation occurs in two different languages. (As you will see in Chapter 7, computer translation of languages has progressed to the point where quite decent results can be obtained, so this is not really an example of a science-fiction application.)

The Dutch firm Royal Dirkzwager has developed a system that tracks the movement of ships around the globe in real-time. It uses a satellite-based technology to track the position of ships on a minute by minute basis. It allows ships to be directed to ports that have space, reduces the time that a ship has to wait to berth, and reduces the amount of fuel that a ship requires.

All these examples have arisen from ingenuity allied with the miniaturization and the reduction of fabrication costs of the computer that I detailed in Chapter 2. They are just a small snapshot of the way that, unless you are a hermit, you will encounter computers in a variety of forms during a single day.

When writing this book, I took short walks of around forty minutes around my village: I find that it clears my head and gives me time to think. One of the walks is along quite a lonely track in the country around my house. During August, I walked along the track trying to think of circumstances when I was not in contact with a computer; I was beginning to think that this walk was one of the few examples. It wasn't: as I passed a gap in a hedge I noticed a combine harvester working in the distance. Such harvesters use sophisticated computer control to regulate the forward speed of the harvester and to keep the rotation speed of the threshing drum constant: this is quite a tricky thing to do and researchers in electrical engineering departments are still trying to develop techniques to optimize the threshing efficiency. Perhaps if I lived at the South Pole? Even there it would be difficult to get away from computers: scientists use computer tags to track the movement of penguins.

What is clear is that everywhere we go, we come into contact with computers and, increasingly, they have altered our lives. For example, a recent study by researchers at the University of California, San Diego, has estimated the amount of information delivered to us every day is equivalent to something like 100,000 words of text. In this chapter I shall be looking at how this information overload affects scientists, examining some positive aspects of computer ubiquity in health-care, and signposting some problems associated with privacy and confidentiality.

Computer ubiquity

There are a number of trends which have liberated the computer from the PC. The first is the increasing miniaturization of electrical components – not just hardware processors and memory, but also communication circuits and circuits used for signal monitoring. The second is the growth of technologies that enable wireless communication between computers. The third, and one that is often overlooked, is the increase in the ruggedness of electronic circuits: I have dropped my mobile phone so many times and yet it still functions.

Ruggedness means that computers can be attached virtually anywhere and still function, even in the most extreme conditions; for example, climate change researchers have attached computer-based measuring instruments to cargo ships and oil tankers in order to measure the temperature of the ocean as they carry out their journeys – such computers are battered by waves, have to undergo major variations of temperature, and suffer from engine vibrations, but still function.

Computers are everywhere: in iPods, mobile phones, security systems, car navigation devices, ATMs, automotive-electronic circuits, and so on. This has three major implications. The first implication is that it gives rise to a new discipline of ambient informatics in which data are available anywhere and at any time.

The second implication is that since these data are generated by our normal interactions in the world, for example by visiting a shop which senses a computer-based device that we may be carrying or a device embedded in, say, a pair of spectacles, or by driving to some destination using an intelligent satellite navigation system, there are major implications in terms of privacy and security.

The third implication concerns the mode of interaction. I interact with my PC in an artificial way in which I am always aware that there is a form of interaction going on. Ubiquitous computing involves an interaction that, in a sense, is natural because it is unobtrusive. Here's an example. One of the first applications of ubiquitous computing was associated with physical security and involved a computer being embedded within an identity badge known as an 'active badge'. The computer emits signals which are picked up by monitoring points in a building and provides information to staff about where colleagues or visitors are. Wearing an active badge is unobtrusive: you don't feel the wireless signals being emitted. It is less obtrusive than your heartbeat which, very occasionally, you are aware of.

In order to examine some of these implications, it is worth focusing on an ambient technology that is mature and cheap, and for which there are a number of working applications.

Radio Frequency Identification

Radio Frequency Identification, or RFID as it is more commonly known, involves the attachment of a small – they can be incredibly small (researchers at Bristol University have attached RFID devices to ants) – electronic device to an object or person. The RFID device, a tag, emits radio waves which can then be picked up by a computer equipped with a radio receiver. RFID tags were initially used in stock control where a retailer such as a supermarket attached them to items of inventory in order to track sales and stock levels.

These tags now retail for a few pence and their use has moved from the domain of stock control. For example, RFID tags are used in hospitals to track down equipment that may be required urgently; they can be attached to young babies or patients who suffer from dementia in order to discover their current location; they can be used as a repository for medical information: when a patient enters hospital they might be given a tag attached to a wristband so that when they, for example, attend some medical test the values of the test can be downloaded to the tag immediately; they can be used for timing participants in a sport such as track athletics; and they represent a potential technology that can be used within intelligent traffic management systems where they would be attached to cars.

Clearly, RFID tags have a major potential but there is a downside: that of privacy. There have been a number of boycotts of RFID-identified products over the fact that RFID tags affixed to products remain operational after the products have been purchased and can be used for surveillance and other purposes. A typical worry was expressed by California State Senator Debra Bowen at a privacy hearing:

> How would you like it if, for instance, one day you realized your underwear was reporting on your whereabouts?

Clearly, an RFID tag attached to the packaging of an item of food poses few privacy concerns: when the item is eaten the wrapping is normally disposed of. However, tags attached to devices such as mobile phones and MP3 players and to other items such as clothes, in conjunction with wireless readers situated in shopping malls, toll roads and other public places, provide the technological infrastructure for a surveillance society.

However, such tags could be very useful when an item is taken into a repair shop. One suggestion that addresses this and privacy concerns is to have a tag that has a section that can be ripped off when the item is bought and which contains the wireless transmitter part of the tag, leaving basic data that could only be read by a hand-held reader that would only be effective a few centimetres away.

Privacy concerns have also been expressed over the potential use of RFID tags that can be inserted into the human body. A company known as Verichip developed an RFID tag that can be surgically implanted into a human. The chip was approved by the American Food and Drug Administration. Clearly, there are some applications of this type of tag, for example carrying out continual monitoring of vital functions such as blood pressure; however, its wide-scale use raises major issues about privacy.

RFID represents the most advanced deployment of ubiquitous computing ideas. However, there are many others which are almost as advanced or over the horizon; it is worth looking at some of them.

Health

One of the major trends in this century has been the increasing amount of integration that has occurred, with the computer carrying out the role of a data processor and synchronizer between the hardware components. The best example of this is the iPhone, which functions as a mobile phone, personal organizer, MP3 player, and Internet access device.

In an article in the *New York Times* (5 November 2009), the columnist David Pogue describes how he was asked to speak at the TED Med conference for 18 minutes on medical applications for the iPhone. TED conferences are organized by a non-profit-making organization which has as its main aim the spreading of ideas (their web site, http://www.ted.com/, is fantastic and contains videos of most of the presentations).

Pogue was worried that he would not find many applications to talk about and he would not fill the 18 minutes. The problem that he did encounter was that he found far too many: over 7,000 applications – just for the iPhone. For the normal user, these included Uhear, an application which enabled the iPhone to test someone's hearing; ProLoQuo2Go, a speech synthesizer for people with speech difficulties that enables the user to touch phrases, icons, and words on the screen of the iPhone and then speaks the text that they have identified; and Retina, an application that allows a colour-blind user to point their iPhone at some coloured item which would then identify the colour.

Pogue also discovered applications for medical staff. These included Anatomy Lab, a virtual cadaver targeted at medical students that allows the user to explore human anatomy; Epocrates, an electronic encyclopaedia which, for example, would warn a doctor about the side effects that two prescribed drugs might have; and AirStrip OB, which, for example, enables an obstetrician to monitor a pregnant mother's vital signs remotely.

Ubiquitous computing also has major applications in the care of the elderly. At an international conference on the use of ubiquitous technology for assistive care, four researchers from the computer science department at the University of Texas, described the design of a simple and cheap wireless network that could be deployed in care homes or the homes of the elderly. This is similar to the use of the iPot detailed earlier that monitors the state of elderly Japanese in their homes.

The network they described would support the sort of monitoring that could easily implement a wide variety of applications, ranging from detecting movement and issuing a message to a remote monitoring station when no movement was detected after a certain time period, to the monitoring of vital signs such as heart rate using RFID technologies. One of the major expansion areas in consumer electronics over the next decade will be that of wireless-based home entertainment where all the wired connections would be replaced by wireless connections. The sort of network described by the researchers could be easily piggy-backed on top of these local networks.

The global panopticon

Computers can be placed in a variety of places: in satellites, in remote telescopes, in temperature measuring systems and even attached to cargo ships. The last decade has seen a major increase in the amount of data that has become available to researchers in areas such as geology, climatology, and physical geography.

There are a large number of examples of computers embedded within hardware that generates huge quantities of data. The Australian Square Kilometre Array of telescopes will generate billions of items of data, the Pan-STARRS array of celestial telescopes will generate several petabytes of data per day, and the technology of gene sequencing is quickly advancing to the point that billions of items of DNA data can be generated in just a few days.

The output from such computers is hugely valuable and has, for example, transformed our study of climate change. However, while the computer has provided the gift of such data, it has posed major problems. The data provided by equipment such as nuclear colliders, gene sequencers, and radio telescopes are of value to the whole scientific community – not just those who have carried out experiments using this hardware. Unfortunately, there are very few standards for the storage and presentation of such data.

There are a small number of scientific data libraries in the world. A good example is the San Diego Supercomputer Center at the University of California, San Diego. Here a large amount of data (currently many petabytes) including bio-informatics and water-resource experiments is stored in such a way that other researchers can access it. Another example is the Australian National Data Service (ANDS), which offers a registration service for data. ANDS does not store data, it stores information about data stored elsewhere: the web site where it can be accessed, the nature of the data, and who was responsible for the generation of the data are just three items that can be accessed via the ANDS computers.

It is not just the amount of data that is increasing, but also the research literature. Medical research is a good example of the explosion. In 1970, there were approximately 200,000 research articles catalogued; this had risen to close on 800,000 by 2009.

During the writing of an early draft of this chapter a major security incident affected the Climatic Research Institute (CRU) of the University of East Anglia. CRU is one of the premier climate research institutes in the world and was responsible for a number of databases including one that contained data from temperature measuring stations around the world.

In October 2009, hackers took a massive file of emails, documents, and program descriptions from one of the computers at the CRU. This theft occurred a few weeks before a major climate change conference in Copenhagen and the contents of the files that were taken caused a blizzard of blog postings, articles, and emails. At its height, I counted over 30 million references to 'Climategate', as it came to be known.

Climategate had a number of dimensions. There were arguments about whether scientists at CRU had massaged data, whether the behaviour of the scientists at CRU was ethical with respect to other scientists who did not share their views about global warming, and whether the United Kingdom's Freedom of Information Act had been violated.

What was clear, however, from this incident was the diverse nature of climate data throughout the world, the lack of proper cataloguing at the various repositories of the data, and the lack of visible program code that manipulated the data.

If the scientific world is to make any headway in terms of fully harnessing the data-gathering and data-processing of computers, then a major shift is required comparable to the political, intellectual, and scientific efforts that created the multi-disciplinary teams that came together for the Manhattan Project or the Bletchley code-breaking projects that had a major effect on the outcome of the Second World War.

Foremost amongst those pressing for the use of the Internet as an open repository of scientific data was Jim Gray, a researcher at Microsoft. He was a computer science researcher who pressed hard for the scientific community to come to terms with the change that computers are bringing to their research. He envisaged a fourth paradigm which would sit alongside the existing three scientific paradigms of empirical observation, analytic processing of the data (usually using statistical methods), and simulation or modelling based on the analysis whereby theories associated with the phenomenon that generated the data are created or modified. Gray's fourth paradigm has a number of components which give rise to both technical and political challenges.

The first is that of the curation of experimental data. This involves the development of Internet sites dedicated to the storage of data, metadata, and any computer programs that are associated with the data, for example a program that carried out some manipulation of the data before it was deposited in a database. This is a major challenge: it does not just involve storing a large quantity of data on a web site, but also involves the specification of metadata – data that describe what each individual collection of data means – for example, the fact that a series of readings was taken from a particular temperature-measuring station between two dates. It also involves storing the details of how the data were changed and the processes and programs used to effect the change.

The second aspect of Gray's fourth paradigm has to do with the explosion of research publications. If you look at the structure of a research paper, you will see references to other papers, references to data sets, and to computer programs. Increasingly, the amount of intellectual effort required to read and digest such papers is approaching overload.

Researchers are starting to address this problem. One way to help the reader is by a form of enhancement whereby supporting materials are added to a raw article. An example of a tool that does this is EMBL Germany's *Reflect* tool. It tags gene, protein, and small molecule names within a research paper, with the tags being hyperlinked to the relevant sequence, structure, or interaction databases that hold the bio-informatic data. So, if a reader wants to cross-reference a gene sequence, all they have to do is to click a link within the paper.

A third component of Gray's fourth paradigm is that of data visualization. When you have a large quantity of data, you will have a lesser but still large quantity of output results after those data have been processed. Increasingly, the size of such output is defeating conventional ways of display such as two-dimensional graphs. Researchers are now striving to develop novel – often three-dimensional – ways of rendering the output such that the viewer can, for example, discern patterns.

The fourth component of Gray's fourth paradigm is the integration of all the elements that make up a computer-based scientific experiment. When you carry out an experiment, you start with a conceptual view of what the experiment will do, you then transform this into a concrete procedure involving the gathering of data, you then process the data using some computer program which displays the results, and, in the final step, you publish the results in some academic journal or conference. What is needed is a chronicle which describes every step in this process, together with a link to all the relevant documents, data, and program codes used in the experiment. This is, without a doubt, the greatest challenge facing those scientists who involve a computer in their experimentation.

Chapter 4
The global computer

Introduction

In this section, I hope I will convince you that to think of the computer as the box that resides on a desk or as a lump of silicon that is used in control and monitoring applications such as those found in avionics applications and chemical plant monitoring is restrictive. I hope that I can convince you that by connecting computers – their processors and their memory – together we can, in fact, create larger computers; the ultimate instantiation of this being the Internet.

The key to the development of the global computer is its processor: an electronic circuit that reads, decodes, and executes the instructions in a computer program and carries out the intentions of the programmer. The speed of computers has increased by orders of magnitude over the last 50 years. As soon as computer technology advances in terms of performance (processor speed, size of memory, and memory-access speed), new applications come along which require even more speed, larger memory, or faster access to the memory, or there is a demand for an improvement in a current application such as weather forecasting, where hardware advances have made predictions more accurate and enabled the forecasters to reach out further into the future.

Wicked problems

Before looking at how we create more and more powerful computers, it is worth looking at some of the major problems they have to solve – so called 'wicked problems' that require huge computational resources for their solution. The world is full of problems that are wicked; they require huge amounts of computer resource and human ingenuity to solve. One of these was the Human Genome Project. This project discovered genetic sequences. If the sequences obtained were to be stored in books, then approximately 3,300 large books would be needed to store the complete information. The computational resources required to search the gene database to look for genes that predispose someone to a particular disease or condition are massive and require supercomputers.

The follow-on projects are progressing slowly since the computational demands are huge and can only be satisfied by the supercomputers that I describe later in this chapter, but it is progressing. There are, however, a class of problems that are incapable of being solved exactly by the computer. They are known as 'NP-hard problems'.

One of the surprising features of many of these problems is that they are simple to describe. Here's an example known as the set partition problem. It involves deciding whether partitioning a set of numbers into two subsets such that the sum of the numbers in each set are equal to each other can be achieved. For example, the set

(1, 3, 13, 8, 6, 11, 4, 17, 12, 9)

can be partitioned into the two sets

(13, 8, 9, 12)

and

(4, 17, 6, 1, 3, 11)

each of which adds up to 42. This looks easy, and it is – for small sets.

However, for much larger sets, for example sets containing tens of thousands of numbers, the time taken to carry out the processing required to discover whether the sets can be split is prohibitive; it rapidly reaches the point where, with even the most powerful computers that have been constructed, the time would exceed the known life of the universe.

Such problems are not academic: they often arise from practical applications; for example, NP-hard problems arise in the design of VLSI circuits, the analysis of genetic sequences, and in avionics design. One of the most famous NP-hard problems is known as the travelling salesman problem and arose from a task associated with the design of computer hardware. Here the aim is, given a series of cities and the distances between them, to develop a route for someone (the travelling salesman) that takes them to each city at the same time as minimizing the route and hence the amount of petrol used.

In practice, the vast majority of NP-hard problems do not require an exact solution – a solution close to the exact solution would do. For example, there is an NP-hard problem known as the bin-packing problem where the computer is given a number of containers and a series of boxes and the aim is to minimize the amount of slack space in the containers. For this problem, it is possible to get within 99.5% of an optimal solution.

Because of this, a large amount of research connected with NP-hardness concerns what are known as approximate algorithms. These, as the name suggests, are descriptions of computer programs that produce approximate but good enough solutions.

Solving wicked problems by software

Recently software researchers have harnessed a number of ideas in biology to improve the capabilities of programs that try to produce approximate solutions. One of these is genetic programming. Here a set of candidate programs are generated to solve the problem and then run. The top programs in terms of efficiency are then collected together as a new generation of programs and combined together to create a further generation of programs. This generation is then run and further mating occurs until a suitable program that works efficiently emerges.

The term 'genetic programming' comes from the fact that the process of generating more and more efficient programs mimics the Darwinian process of evolution (genetic programming is often known as evolutionary programming). In common with the other techniques I detail in this section, it requires considerable computer resources.

There are a number of other techniques that mimic biological processes in order to solve wicked problems. Swarm computing is based on a model that draws on behaviour exhibited by birds within a flock, insects cooperating with each other over a task such as food gathering, or fish swimming in a shoal. Such behaviour can be modelled in very simple ways and this simplicity has been transferred to a number of optimization programs.

There are also computer programs that mimic the behaviour of social insects such as ants, for example, processing data in the same way that ants forage for food or dispose of their dead. The problems that such ant-colony programs solve are concerned with an area known as routing; here the underlying data can be modelled as a series of points connected by lines, for example the layout of connections on a VLSI-fabricated chip.

There are also other ways of programming wicked problems. There is a controversial area of computer science known as

5. The CRAY XM-P48

artificial intelligence – controversial because of the over-claiming that its proponents have made over the last thirty years. Researchers in this area belong to two camps: those who try to use the computer to gain an understanding of how humans carry out processes such as reasoning and those who just want to develop intelligent software artefacts whose performance matches that of humans – irrespective of whether the software bears any resemblance to human processes.

The artefact builders have developed a number of techniques that have been successful in the real world. Almost certainly the best known product of this approach to artificial intelligence is 'Deep Blue', a chess-playing program that defeated the world chess champion Gary Kasparov in 1997.

This program relied on the massive calculating power of a supercomputer and did not base much of its power on studies of how human chess players behaved. There are however a number of artificial intelligence programs that attempt to overcome wickedness by a combination of brute computational force and human heuristics. One type of program is known as an expert system. It attempts to carry out tasks that humans carry out such as diagnosing illnesses or finding hardware faults in electronic systems. Such expert systems rely not only on the computer's power but also on an encoding of some of the heuristics used by human experts in the domain they work in.

Even given the advances in software technology that we have seen over the last twenty years there is still a need for powerful computers: the software technology goes some distance to solving big problems – but not far enough – and there is the natural tendency to move on and attack bigger problems and more complicated problems. So, the last 40 years has seen major advances in supercomputing.

Supercomputers

The first computers had a single hardware processor that executed individual instructions. It was not too long before researchers started thinking about computers that had more than one processor. The simple theory here was that if a computer had n processors then it would be n times faster. Before looking at the topic of supercomputers, it is worth debunking this notion.

If you look at many classes of problems for which you feel supercomputers could have been used, you see that a strictly linear increase in performance is not achieved. If a problem that is solved by a single computer is solved in 20 minutes, then you will find a dual processor computer solving it in perhaps 11 minutes. A 3-processor computer may solve it in 9 minutes, and a 4-processor computer in 8 minutes. There is a law of diminishing returns; often, there comes a point when adding a processor slows down the computation. What happens is that each processor needs to communicate with the others, for example passing on the result of a computation; this communicational overhead becomes bigger and bigger as you add processors to the point when it dominates the amount of useful work that is done.

The sort of problems where they are effective is where a problem can be split up into sub-problems that can be solved almost independently by each processor with little communication.

The history of supercomputing can be split into two phases: the 1970s and the 1980s and the years after these two decades. Before looking at the history, it will be instructive to see how speeds of supercomputers have increased over the last 70 years.

The first real supercomputers were developed by two companies, CDC and Cray. The most successful designs were based on a vector architecture. This is based on a processor that is capable of carrying out a number of instructions on data simultaneously, for example adding a thousand numbers together at the same time. The computers made by the Cray Corporation were the iconic supercomputers. Figure 5 shows a CRAY XM-P48, an example of which was situated at the Organisation Européenne pour la Recherche Nucléaire (CERN). It resembles the sort of furniture designed for the waiting room of a 1980s advertising company. However, when it was delivered to research labs around the world it was the fastest computer in existence: in 1982 it was a state of the art computer it had a theoretical top speed of 800 MFLOPS from both its processors (an MFLOP is a million instructions that carry out some arithmetic operation such as adding two numbers together).

Supercomputers were delivered to a variety of customers including CERN, the Los Alamos National Laboratory in the USA, the Boeing Corporation, the British Meteorological Office, the National Aerospace Laboratory in Japan, the US National Nuclear Security Administration, and the US Department of Energy Laboratory at Oak Ridge.

The customers for such behemoths betray the sort of applications they were used for: nuclear experiment simulations, weather forecasting, simulating the day-to-day processes that occur in a nuclear reactor, and the aerodynamic design of large planes. The key similarities between each of these applications are the volume of computation that needs to be carried out and the fact that most of the computations involve number crunching.

'Vector architecture computers' dominated supercomputing until the 1990s when mass-produced processors started becoming so cheap that it became feasible to connect them together rather than design special-purpose chips. One of the fastest computers in the world is the Cray XT5 Jaguar system which has been installed at the National Center for Computational Sciences in the USA. It has around 19,000 computers and 224,000 processing elements, based on standard hardware processors rather than bespoke designed processors.

Even small-scale research establishments can now get in on the act, often by developing their own version of a supercomputer out of commercial hardware processors. These computers are known as Beowulf clusters. Such computers are based on readily available processors such as the ones you find in your home PC, the LINUX operating system – a free operating system often used by researchers for scientific computation – and other open-source software.

The power of Beowulf computers is huge and they are cheap to make: the Microwulf cluster that was developed by computer science professor Joel Adams and student Tim Brom weighed just 31 pounds (small enough to fit in a suitcase) and had speeds of up to 26 Gflops. The cost of this computer in early 2007 was about $2,500.

In 2009, Intel, the leading chip maker in the world, announced a new processing chip containing 48 separate processors on a single chip. Such chips used in a Beowulf computer would bring real supercomputing power to the desktop.

The Internet as a computer

This chapter started out describing supercomputers: machines that carried out huge numbers of computations. Such computers can employ thousands of processors. What is surprising is that there is a much larger computer and anyone who uses a desktop or laptop computer is part of it. It's the Internet.

The Internet has been described as a network or, more accurately, as a network of networks. Let's see how this works out. When I order an item from an online bookseller such as Amazon, I click on a series of links which identify me and which identify what books I want to buy. Each time I click, a message is sent to a computer at Amazon known as a web server. The computer discovers which page I want and sends it back to me, for example a page containing the final order that I make. I then click on another link – usually the link that informs the bookseller that I have finished my order.

As part of the interaction between my browser and the Amazon web server other computers are used. First, there are the computers that transmit the messages from my computer to the web server – they do not go directly but are split into packets each of which may go via a set of completely different computers.

Second, there is the collection of computers that are known as the Domain Name System (DNS). The DNS is a hugely important part of the Internet. When you type in a symbolic name for a web site, such as http://www.open.ac.uk, it is the DNS that discovers where on the Internet this web site is situated. Without this collection of computers, the Internet would be unable to function.

There are other computers that are involved in the sales process. A book retailer will have a number of computers known as database servers. These contain large collections of data; in the case of the online bookseller, they would hold data such as which books are on sale, their price, and the number in stock. They would also contain data such as past sales to individuals and marketing information, such as the amount of sales for past published books. When the web page that contains details about availability is presented to a customer, then a database server is involved.

There will also be computers at the bookseller's warehouse. One application of such computers is to provide what is known as a picking list: this is a list of books that have been bought within a certain time period. The computer will sort these books into a list that details each book and its position in the warehouse and will organize the list in such a way that the amount of travelling needed by warehouse staff is minimized. There will also be a computer that is used by warehouse staff to inform the database server that books have been picked and need to be marked as being taken from the shelves.

There will also be computers that carry out financial functions, sending money transfers to book suppliers for the books that have been bought from them, and sending debits to credit card companies for the purchases made by the customer. So, what this example shows us is that the Internet functions as a series of computers – or more accurately computer processors – carrying out some task such as buying a book. Conceptually, there is little difference between these computers and the supercomputer, the only difference is in the details: for a supercomputer the communication between processors is via some internal electronic circuit, while for a collection of computers working together on the Internet the communication is via external circuits used for that network.

The idea that network technologies used in the Internet can be used to create a sort of supercomputer has been embedded in something known as the grid and the resulting computer known as the grid computer.

The grid

So, what is grid computing? Well a computer grid is a collection of conventional computers that are linked together using Internet technology and usually connected by high speed communication circuits. There are two ways of looking at the grid: that it is the continuation of mainstream supercomputing ideas – this is the view taken by researchers – or that it is a new way of optimizing the use of computers in an enterprise. You will remember that computer processors have a large amount of slack when they are used: they can be idle for as much as 95% of the time. The vendors of commercial grid software make the point that buying their product will reduce an enterprise's hardware costs by a significant amount.

Grids can be formal or informal; the former is usually supported by commercial software which maintains the grid, allowing file sharing and processor sharing, the latter is a loose confederation of computers that carry out some large task. A good example of an informal network is folding@home. This is a network that is coordinated by the Stanford University Chemistry department. Its aim is to carry out much of the number crunching associated with protein folding; this is work associated with the Human Genome Project and which attempts to find cures for serious diseases such as Parkinson's Disease and Cystic Fibrosis. The network has hundreds of thousands of computers connected to it with a combined speed approaching 4 pFLOPS.

Grid computing represents a subtle shift from the idea of a supercomputer carrying out a massive number of calculations in order to solve a wicked problem towards commercial applications outside the realm of number crunching. In application terms, it has influenced the idea known as cloud computing which regards the Internet as a central utility for all applications – not just number crunching – and which threatens to overturn the current way that computers are used commercially. I will discuss this further in Chapter 7.

Afterword

What this chapter has shown is that to think of a computer as just a box sitting on a desk or as a piece of silicon-based circuitry in something like a DVD player or a set of traffic lights is too limited: that regarding the Internet as a large computer raises a host of interesting questions which I will address in Chapter 7, there I discuss an evolving model of commercial computer use that takes much of the processing and data away from individual computers and delegates it to powerful servers maintained by commercial enterprises.

This is also a theme I shall look at in the final chapter, where I will examine the work of Jonathan Zittrain and Nicholas Carr. Zittrain has posited that the freewheeling growth of the Internet has enabled a new age of creativity amongst computer users, but at a cost in terms of problems such as security. His book *The Future of the Internet* describes a possible scenario where commercial pressures close down much of what the ordinary computer user can do to the point where the home computer is relegated to something like the dumb terminal of the 1960s and when a golden age of computational creativity ends.

Carr uses the analogy of the Internet as a computer but concentrates on an industrial viewpoint. He posits a future where computing power becomes a utility in the same way that electrical power becomes a utility and where the role of the computer – at least for the home owner – is reduced to that of accessing the Internet. I shall return to this theme in the final chapter.

Chapter 5
The insecure computer

Introduction

During the 2009 Iranian election protests, foreign activists disabled the computers acting as web servers and belonging to the Iranian government by carrying out what is known as a denial of service attack. The attack took place as part of the protests against what many saw as a corrupt election result. The activists flooded the servers with hundreds of thousands of requests for web pages to the point where the processors of the web servers were overwhelmed by the amount of data being sent. This effectively closed them down.

In 1999, a computer virus known as Melissa was released into the Internet. What the virus did was to infect the Outlook email program which formed part of the Windows operating system. The virus was spread using email. If someone received an email that contained the virus as an attachment and then clicked on the attachment, their computer would be infected. Once a computer was infected by the virus, it accessed the contact list of Outlook and emailed the first 50 contacts on this list and sent the virus to them. This was a particularly pernicious virus, not just because it spread rapidly, but because it also had the potential to modify word-processed documents on an infected computer so that they also spread the virus.

In 2007, the British government reported that child benefit data for over 25 million people entrusted to Her Majesty's Revenue and Customs department had been lost. The details were stored on two CDs which were sent in the post to another department.

These are just three examples of computer insecurity. The first two involved technical failings while the last was a managerial failing. The aim of this chapter is to look at the threats to computers and how they can be countered. It will also look at some of the entwined issues of privacy.

Viruses and malware

A virus is a computer program that is introduced into a computer or a network of computers illegally; once introduced it carries out some malicious act. Typical malicious acts include: deleting files; in the case of the Melissa virus, emailing documents out to other Internet users; monitoring the keystrokes carried out by a user in order to discover important information such as passwords and banking information; and scrambling a file so that it becomes unreadable and then asking for a ransom which, when the victim pays, will result in an email being sent to the victim with instructions on how to unscramble the file. Viruses are a subset – albeit a large subset – of a collection of software known as malware.

There are three main ways for a virus to be introduced into a computer system. The first is as an attachment, for example a user may be sent an email which contains a message about the surprising behaviour of a celebrity with instructions to click on the attachment in order to see photographic evidence of the behaviour; as soon as the recipient of the email clicks on the attachment the virus will have taken up residence on the computer.

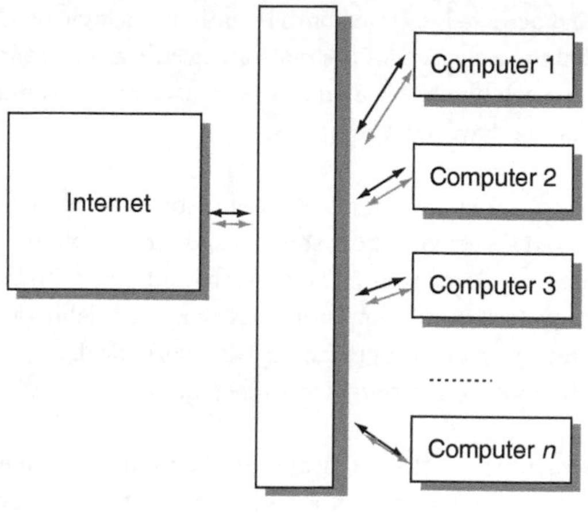

6. The architecture of a firewall

The second way that a computer catches a virus is by using insecure software. There is a host of free software available on the Internet; most of it is useful (I use an excellent program for backing up my files), however, some software will contain viruses. As soon as the software that contains the virus is installed, the virus is installed as well. The carrier of the virus is often known as a 'Trojan horse'.

The third way is by not employing or not properly employing a program known as a firewall. This is a barrier that prevents unwanted connections into a computer. It continually monitors these connections and rejects any that are deemed to be harmful.

There are a number of other types of malware apart from viruses and Trojan horses. A logic bomb is a program that executes within a computer when a particular condition occurs, for example when a file is first accessed. A time bomb is similar to a logic bomb except that the execution of the malware occurs at some time in the future. Such bombs have mainly been used by disgruntled employees who have left a company.

A trapdoor is a weakness in a computer system that allows unauthorized access into the system. Trapdoors are often associated with poorly written systems that interact with the operating system of the computer, but can also be deliberately constructed by system programmers who work for the organization whose computers are affected.

A worm is a program that replicates itself a number of times across a network. One of the first intrusions that were associated with the Internet was the Morris Worm which affected a large number of computers in the emerging Internet.

A rabbit is similar to a worm except that it replicates itself on one computer rather than a network and effectively shuts down the computer by hogging all its resources – main memory, file storage memory, or even the hardware processor can be affected.

Viruses can be hidden in a number of locations, for example they can be integrated with programs: they can surround a program and intercept any requests for the program to be carried out, they can be appended to the end of a program, or they can be embedded within a program. They can also be embedded within a document or an image and then executed when the document or image is opened.

An important technology that is used to detect, isolate, and delete viruses is the virus scanner. There are a number of commercial and free virus scanners that are available via companies such as Norton, Kaspersky, and AVG. A virus is just a program – albeit a program that can cause major destructive effects – and like all programs has a signature. This is the pattern of zeroes and ones that is unique to the virus. A virus scanner will, when executed, process the hard disk and memory of a computer looking for virus signatures. In order to do this, it relies on a database of signatures of known viruses.

When you purchase a virus scanner, you also purchase a database of virus signatures and a program that periodically updates the database as new viruses are discovered and examined by the company that has sold you the scanner.

Pfleeger and Pfleeger in their excellent book on computer security, which is cited at the end of this book, describe the steps that you need to take in order to protect yourself from viruses: use virus scanners; use only commercial software that has been purchased from reputable vendors; test all new software that you are suspicious of on an isolated computer; if you receive an email with an attachment then only open it if you know that it is safe (one check is to type some of the key words of the email into a search engine such as Google: you may possibly find that someone has flagged the email as hazardous); and always backup your files, for example moving them to a cheap hard disk that is normally kept separate from your computer.

Another technology – already briefly referred to – that is highly effective against virus and other attacks is the firewall. There are a variety of firewall architectures. One architecture is shown in Figure 6. What a firewall does is to intercept any traffic from outside a protected network – usually from the Internet – and reject any traffic that can be dangerous for the network. There is also a firewall known as a personal firewall that protects individual computers; however, its function is similar to an industrial firewall: it's just that it has a smaller set of functions. Such firewalls are normally marketed for home use and are sold as an integrated package that contains a virus scanner and other security software.

Typical actions a firewall carries out are: checking any attachments to see if they contain viruses, denying access to a computer or a network to messages sent from a computer that has been identified as the source of hazardous traffic, and denying facilities to external computers such as copying files.

Computer crime

There are a large number of crimes associated with the computer, including: fraud achieved by the manipulation of computer records; in some countries, spamming, the sending of unrequested emails usually selling some product or service, is illegal; accessing a computer system without permission; accessing a computer system in order to read, modify, and delete data without permission; stealing data or software; industrial espionage carried out via a computer; stealing the identity of someone by accessing their personal details; accessing financial data and stealing funds associated with that data; spreading viruses; and distributing child pornography.

A typical non-technical crime is where an employee has access to a financial system and issues a number of cheques payable to themselves and/or others. Such crimes have often involved figures of over a million dollars before the perpetrator was caught.

In 2008, a job vacancy was posted on a web site that contained adverts for translators. The job involved correcting texts which had been translated into English from another language. Applicants were asked to provide data such as that normally found on a CV, plus their bank account details. The 'company' that issued the advert was connected to a crime syndicate in the Ukraine. Anyone who applied would have their account siphoned of cash and then used for a money-laundering scam.

In 2009, a survey of American computers discovered that many millions of computers in the United States were 'infected' with fake security software. This is the result of a very sophisticated scam in which, when a computer user visited a particular site, they saw an alert in a pop-up window that told them that they had a virus infection and that free software could easily be downloaded and be used to detect and remove the virus along with many others. The software was, of course, a virus that was capable of discovering financial details of the user of the computer.

In 2006, three Russian hackers were jailed for eight years for carrying out an attack known as a denial of service attack on British bookmakers. In this type of attack, a computer is flooded with messages – sometime they are requests for web pages and sometimes they are email messages – with the result that the computer that is attacked is disabled and cannot respond to normal users' requests. The hackers targeted the web server of a major online bookmaker, who refused to pay a large ransom, their computer was blocked during the Breeders' Cup races, and the company lost more than £160,000 for each day of the attack.

An important point to make about computer crime is that many crimes can be carried out by computer users who have little technical knowledge. The examples above require varying degrees of technical skill with the money-siphoning example requiring the least. Typical non-technical crimes include: rummaging through large refuse bins for computer printouts containing sensitive information (a process known as dumpster diving), taking a photograph of important information about a computer system written on a white board using a mobile phone, and stealing a password and using that password to masquerade as the user of a computer system.

All these non-technical examples require, at most, the sort of computer knowledge that you gain by using a home computer for word processing or spreadsheet work. It is no surprise, then, given that computer crime can be carried out in a technical or non-technical way, that there is a variety of technical and non-technical defences against computer crime.

Technical defences against computer crime

One of the major defences against the large number of computer-related, technical crimes is cryptography. This is a technology used to hide and scramble data – data that may be stored in a computer or may be in transit between two computers connected by a network. Cryptography has been around since Roman times when Julius Caesar used it to send messages to his military commanders. The ciphers that are used in computing are quite complicated; however, a description of the Caesar cipher will give you a rough idea of how they work.

The Caesar cipher involves changing a text by replacing each letter in a message by the *n*th letter forward from it in the alphabet. For example, if *n* was two then the letter 'a' would be transformed to the letter 'c'; letters at the end of the alphabet would be transformed into letters at the beginning, for example the letter 'y' would be transformed to 'a'.

> Caesar was here

would be transformed to

> Ecguct ycu jgtg

In the Caesar cipher, the number *n* acted as a password. In cryptography circles, it is known as the key: it was used to determine the precise transformation that was applied to the text that was scrambled (the plain text) in order to produce the text that could not be read (the cipher text). All that would be required of the recipient of the message above would be to know the key (the number of places each letter was transformed forward). They would then be able to extract the message from the cipher text.

The Caesar cipher is very simple and can be easily cracked. Cracking modern ciphers is a complicated business that requires a knowledge of statistics to understand. It requires data about word frequency, letter frequency, and, ideally, some knowledge of the context of the email and of some possible words that could be contained in the message. It was knowledge of phrases that could appear in a message that enabled cryptographers in the Second World War to decipher German messages. For example, many of the messages would contain the words 'Heil Hitler'.

We have come a long way since the Caesar cipher; indeed, a long way since the Second World War. Computer-based ciphers are still based on substitutions such as the type found in the Caesar cipher. However, two factors have enabled ciphers to become very much stronger. The first is that transpositions are applied to the plain text as well as substitutions; a transposition being the movement of a character in the text to another position in the text. The second is that a huge number of substitutions and transpositions are carried out, normally via computer hardware or very efficient computer programs.

The type of cipher that I have described is known as a symmetric cipher; it is symmetric because the same key would be used for changing the plain text (encrypting it) as for transforming the cipher text back to the plain text (decrypting it). Symmetric encryption methods are very efficient and can be used to scramble large files or long messages being sent from one computer to another.

Unfortunately, symmetric techniques suffer from a major problem: if there are a number of individuals involved in a data transfer or in reading a file, each has to know the same key. This makes it a security nightmare. It is exacerbated by the fact that the more complex a key, the less likely it is for a message to be read; consequently, a key such as 'Darrel' is useless, while a key such as

55Tr3e343E4((!!dfg21AVD90kk - 9jk}

provides a high degree of security, the only problem being that it can be very difficult to remember and would need to be stored somewhere such as a wallet or within a drawer in a desk.

While there have been a number of attempts at making the key distribution process secure, for example by encoding keys on biometric smart cards and devising secure protocols for the distribution of a key or set of keys, key security for symmetric encryption and decryption still remains a problem.

One public solution to this problem was developed by three American computer science researchers, Whitfield Diffie, Ralph Merkle, and Martin Hellman, with a practical implementation of their ideas by three other researchers: Ronald Rivest, Adi Shamir, and Leonard Adleman. I use the word 'public' since declassified documents from the British government indicate that three British researchers, Clifford Cocks, Malcolm Williamson, and James Ellis, were also developing work in this area at GCHQ, the British government's top-secret communications headquarters in Cheltenham. Their work was carried out in the early 1970s.

The solution that was developed by these researchers was known as public key cryptography or asymmetric cryptography. At its heart, it relies on the inability of computers to solve difficult problems that require massive computational resources. The term 'asymmetric' best describes the technique, as it requires two keys, a public key and a private key, that are different.

Let us assume that two computer users *A* and *B* wish to communicate using asymmetric cryptography and each has a public key and a private key. The public key is published by each of the two users. If *A* wants to send an encrypted message to *B*, then she will use *B*'s public key to encrypt the message. When *B* receives the message, he will then use his private key to decrypt the message. Asymmetric cryptographic systems have a number of properties; a very important one is that the public key that is used to send the message cannot be used by someone who intercepts the message in order to decode it.

At a stroke, public key cryptography removed a major problem associated with symmetric cryptography: that of a large number of keys in existence some of which may be stored in an insecure way. However, a major problem with asymmetric cryptography is the fact that it is very inefficient (about 10,000 times slower than symmetric cryptography): while it can be used for short messages such as email texts, it is far too inefficient for sending gigabytes of data. However, as you will see later, when it is combined with symmetric cryptography, asymmetric cryptography provides very strong security.

One strong use is to provide a form of digital identity as a digital signature in which the mathematical properties of the key generation process are used to provide authentication that the person who purports to have sent a message is, in fact, that person.

A second use is in sending secure messages, for example between a bank and a customer. Here the identity of a user and the web server is mediated by a digital identity check. It is worth saying here that you should not rely solely on technology, but use common sense. For example a popular fraud is to send a user an email purporting to be from a bank asking them to check into a rogue site which masquerades as the bank site and extracts out account data that is used for siphoning funds. The Internet is full of villains who are experts in subverting the technology.

There are a number of technologies that are used to provide this security; almost all are based on a combination of symmetric and asymmetric cryptography. One very popular security scheme is known as the Secure Sockets Layer – normally shortened to SSL. It is based on the concept of a one-time pad. This gives an almost ideal cryptographic scheme. It requires the sender and receiver to have a document known as a pad which contains thousands of random characters. The sender takes the first *n* characters, say 50, and then encrypts the message using them as the key. The receiver, when they receive the message, takes the fifty characters from their pad and decrypts the message. Once these characters are used for the key, they are discarded and the next message is sent using the next *n* characters.

A major advantage of the one-time pad is that once a password is used it is discarded; another advantage is that any document can be used to generate a key; for example, a telephone directory or a novel could equally well be used. The main disadvantage of a one-time pad is that they require synchronization between the sender and receiver and a high degree of security for the printing, distribution, and storage of the keys.

SSL uses public key cryptography to communicate the randomly generated key between the sender and receiver of a message. This key is only used once for the data interchange that occurs and, hence, is an electronic analogue of a one-time pad. When each of the parties to the interchange has received the key, they encrypt and decrypt the data employing symmetric cryptography, with the generated key carrying out these processes. If the two parties want a further interchange of data, then another key is generated and the transfer proceeds as before.

Another technical defence against computer crime is the password. The theory behind passwords is simple: that the user of a computer remembers some set of characters and uses them to access a web site or a file – the password, in effect, acts as a proxy for the user's identity. Sometimes the password is used as an encryption key. Passwords offers major advantages; however, password schemes can be less secure because of human failings.

In general, computer users choose poor passwords. The best passwords and cryptographic keys are those which are long and which contain alphabetic, numeric, and special characters such as !. For example, the password

s22Akk;;!!9iJ66s0 – iKL69

is an excellent password, while 'John' is a poor one. In the 1990s, the online bank Egg discovered that its customers chose poor passwords. For example, 50% chose family members' names. Charles and Shari Pfleeger, in their excellent book *Security in Computing*, provide sensible advice on password choice: don't just use alphabetic characters, use long passwords, avoid names or words, choose an unlikely password that is memorable such as

Ilike88potatoesnot93carrots!!

change your password regularly, don't write your password down, and never tell anyone else what your password is.

As well as passwords, there are a number of hi-tech ways of identifying yourself to a computer. One area that has attracted a considerable amount of attention is biometric identification. Here, technologies that recognize a computer user from unique physical traits are employed, often in conjunction with passwords. Typical traits that can be used include fingerprints, iris patterns, a user's face, their voice, and the geometry of a hand. Many of the techniques are in the research phase with some having unacceptably high error rates and also being susceptible to attack. For example, an active area of voice technology is to simulate a person's voice from a set of recordings.

Non-technological security

In the advice I quoted from the Pfleeger and Pfleeger book *Security in Computing*, there was the injunction not to tell anyone your password. This is a good example of a precaution against non-technical security breaches and the problems that computer users face over and above those associated with viruses and other illegal technologies.

The former security hacker Kevin Mitnick, in his book *The Art of Deception*, describes a number of attacks on computer systems which require no technical knowledge at all. A number of hackers have used a variety of techniques categorized as social engineering to penetrate a computer system – not by employing worms, viruses or operating system trapdoors, but by taking advantage of human frailties. In his book, he states that social engineering

> ... uses influence and persuasion to deceive people by convincing them that the social engineer is someone he isn't, or by manipulation. As a result, the social engineer is able to take advantage of people to obtain information with or without the use of technology.

Here's a typical social engineering attack decribed by Mitnick. A potential intruder builds up a relationship with the clerk at a video rental store that forms part of a collection of video stores by masquerading as a clerk at another store. The relationship is nurtured for a number of months to the point where the innocent clerk assumes that the person they are talking to actually works at a sister store. Then, one day, the intruder rings up the clerk claiming that their computer is down and asks for details of a customer (name, address, credit card) who wants to borrow a video. Once obtained the customer's bank account can be rifled.

As well as crimes being committed using non-technical means, data have also been lost because of human frailty. The last decade has seen a large number of data leaks from companies and organizations. For example, in 2008, the British banking group HSBC admitted that it had lost data on many tens of thousands of its customers' insurance records. Although the disk was protected by a password, it was not encrypted, leaving it open to anyone with a good level of computing expertise to read it.

In 2007, in one of the largest data leaks in British computing history, the government's Revenue and Customs Department lost 25,000,000 records containing financial and other data belonging to British citizens who were being paid child benefit. An employee had written the details onto computer disks and had sent the disks unrecorded to another government department – they were then lost in the post.

There is an impression amongst the public that the main threats to security and to privacy arise from technological attack. However, the threat from more mundane sources is equally high. Data thefts, damage to software and hardware, and unauthorized access to computer systems can occur in a variety of non-technical ways: by someone finding computer printouts in a waste bin; by a window cleaner using a mobile phone camera to take a picture of a display containing sensitive information; by an office cleaner stealing documents from a desk; by a visitor to a company noting down a password written on a white board; by a disgruntled employee putting a hammer through the main server and the backup server of a company; or by someone dropping an unencrypted memory stick in the street.

To guard a computer against technical attacks is relatively easy: it involves purchasing security software and making sure that the files that the software uses – for example, virus signature files – are up to date. There is, of course, always a struggle between the intruder that uses technical means to access a computer and the staff who are responsible for security. Sometimes an attack succeeds: for example, denial of service attacks in the 1990s was a serious problem, but, very quickly, technical means have been developed to cope with them.

For companies and other organizations, it is much more difficult to guard against non-technical attacks: it requires a whole set of procedures which guard against all possible security risks. Examples of such procedures are those for handling visitors, such as enforcing the rule that they do not wander around a building by themselves; for disposing of waste computer printouts; for ensuring the safety of laptops when travelling; for disposing of old computers that may have sensitive data stored on their hard disks; for prohibiting the publishing of personal details on social web sites that may help social engineering attackers gain access to a computer network; and for ensuring a clean desk policy.

Non-technical security is much more difficult because it is much more pervasive than technical security: it requires the cooperation of everyone from reception area staff to the head of the computer centre, and, in organizations that take security seriously, is embedded in a thick document known as a security manual or manual of security procedures.

For the individual working at home who wants to guard against non-technical attacks, it is much easier. All that is needed is to encrypt any file that is sensitive, for example a spreadsheet containing financial data; employ adequate passwords for any files of sensitive data; never give data such as passwords and bank account numbers over the Internet or in response to a phone call; and, if you do have to carry data around, buy an encrypted memory stick – they used to be somewhat expensive, but have come down in price since they first came on the market.

Chapter 6
The disruptive computer

Borders UK

This morning, as I started writing the first draft of the first chapter of this book, I heard that Borders UK, one of my favourite bookshops, was in financial trouble – four days later, they went into administration. One reason quoted in the BBC news was that the company was finding it very difficult to compete with online retailers such as Amazon. It is much more expensive to run a chain of bookstores, some of which are situated in prime shopping locations, than a warehouse, a web site, and a call centre. Just as a comparison I looked at the price of a book that I bought recently. In a city-centre shop, I would pick it up at £34, while it was currently advertised on the Amazon web site at £20.13.

While the employees of Borders are able to use computers to help them in answering customer queries and ordering out-of-stock items, in the end they have threatened their jobs. I did think that bookstores had something of a future, since they offered browsing facilities, until I saw that a number of booksellers, via a system known as Google preview, allow visitors to their web site to browse the table of contents of a book and many of the pages within the book. *For the book trade, the computer is disruptive.*

My favourite record shop in Milton Keynes was the Virgin Megastore which, after a management buyout, renamed itself Zavvi. Shortly thereafter, the Zavvi retail chain folded. One of the reasons quoted was the availability of cheaper music downloads from sites such as iTunes. Again, the staff at Zavvi found the computer useful in carrying out their jobs, but, in the end, it killed off their trade. *For the music trade, the computer is disruptive.*

I can read the national newspapers from my computer; occasionally I do, but most of the time I access the BBC news site, a site that has won a number of awards for its design, implementation, and content. The increasing availability of news on the Internet has had a dramatic effect on newspaper sales. Newspapers across the Western world have been coping with a slide in advertising revenue, declining circulation, and a movement of readers to free news online. According to the USA Audit Bureau of Circulations, the average daily circulation for 379 daily American newspapers was down 10.62% in the April to September 2009 period, compared with the same period in 2008. The computer has helped the reporters who file copy for their newspapers: word processors are a fantastic piece of software. However, the computer has led to layoffs and staff reductions in many newspapers. *For the newspaper industry, the computer is disruptive.*

Another disruption associated with newspapers is the reduction in the amount of space devoted to reviews – for example, book reviews – and the fact that review staff, both permanent and freelance, are often the first to feel the chill winds of redundancy. Book reviewers and film reviewers used to be very powerful figures: their opinion could kill off a book or film or elevate it in the popular listings. There are now a large number of sites that review films and books. Some of them are just devoted to reviews – a site such as rottentomatoes.com – or provide reviews as part of their business: a good example here is the Amazon web site which, although it is devoted to the selling of a variety of goods, includes reviews of the goods in their catalogue – the reviews being written by customers.

In this section of the book, I shall look at some of the ways that computers have affected us in terms of how we interact with others, in terms of employment, and in terms of how technology is improving our lives; I will also look at some of the ways that might affect us negatively.

Disruptive technologies

One of the key writers about the disruptive effects of technology is Clayton Christensen. His two books, *The Innovator's Dilemma* and *The Innovator's Solution*, look at how technological devices such as the hard disk storage unit can have major effects on industry.

Disruptive innovations can be placed in two classes: low-end disruptive innovations and new-market disruptive innovations. The latter is where a technological advance creates new business opportunities, changes the behaviour of consumers, and often leads to the elimination of industrial sub-sectors. A lower-end disruptive innovation affects current technological objects and services and reduces their price and consequently their availability.

The computer has given rise to disruptions covered by both categories. For example, when the mobile phone was designed and developed the companies that manufactured them added messaging as an afterthought, not thinking that it would be a feature that would be used so much, to the point where it is inconceivable that a mobile telephone would now be sold without text messaging facilities. This is an example of new-market disruption which obliterated much of the pager industry.

An example of a lower-end disruption is that of open-source software which I discuss later in this chapter. This has enabled computer users to use operating systems, word processors, spreadsheet systems, and photo utilities which cost nothing – a true reduction in price.

Open-source development

When you use a computer to access the Internet, you have a possible audience of hundreds of millions of users and a potential to link those users together. Wikipedia is an example of mass collaboration: all the entries have been initiated and edited by volunteers. Another, equally impressive, example is the rise of open-source software. This is software that differs from commercial software in a number of ways; first, it is free; second, the program code of open-source software is available for anyone to read; and – this is where the term 'open source' comes from, 'source' referring to the program code – third, anyone can take the code, modify it, and even sell it as a product.

There is a large quantity of open-source program code in existence; the two most used are Apache and Linux. The former is the software that is used to dispense pages from a web server. Currently, it is estimated that something like 65% of web servers use Apache. Linux is an even more impressive story. It is an operating system, and a competitor to the popular Windows operating system. It has its roots in a simple operating system known as MINIX which was developed by a computer science academic, Andrew Tanenbaum, in order to teach his students about the design of large systems.

Linux was developed by Linus Torvalds, who was a student at the University of Helsinki. He decided to improve on MINIX and started developing Linux, initially inspired by some of the design ideas used for MINIX. The original implementation of Linux was so good that it came to the attention of a number of software developers at the same time that the Internet was blossoming. The result was that the system evolved into being maintained by programmers who devote their time for nothing.

Linux is very impressive in terms of both penetration and in terms of what it offers. A recent survey showed that 80% of the most reliable web-hosting companies used Linux and that it is the operating system of choice for many supercomputers. There is also a desktop version of Linux which contains the usual array of software that you would expect: word processors, graphics programs, image editors, email programs, and audio players.

In desktop terms, Linux still has some distance to go before it threatens the very popular Windows operating system. For example, it is sometimes fiddly to install new software for the desktop version. But it is still the most impressive example of the trend of computer users creating a large, complex artefact outside established institutions.

Advertising

The computer has had a major effect on the revenue earned by both television and newspaper companies. This is mainly down to the use of online adverts, but is also due to the fact that television programmes containing adverts can be recorded and, when wound back, the adverts can be fast-forwarded. The key to the disruption that has occurred in these industries is targeting. This concept is nothing new: all it means is that you place your adverts where you think they will get the maximum readership and payback. For example, if you had an advert for study tours to Greece which involved visiting ancient sites and listening to renowned Greek classicists, then you would probably have targeted the advert at a newspaper such as *The Independent*.

The computer and the Internet have changed the face of targeting and made it more effective. The major technology that has been disruptive is AdWords, a Google technology that earned that company billions of dollars. AdWords is based on what is known as a pay-per-click model. An advertiser who wants their products or services advertised on Google specifies an amount that they will pay when an online advert appears in a page retrieved when someone carries out a Google web search.

The advertiser specifies what keywords will trigger the adverts, so that if a user types the word 'Angling' into the Google search box, they will find, as I did when I typed in the word, that three adverts for online fishing tackle sites were displayed, one advert for fishing holidays displayed, an advert for angling items at Amazon shown, a link to a site that marketed a revolutionary way of throwing fish bait into a river or lake displayed, and a link to a site which collects together links associated with angling displayed.

AdWords represents a much more fine-grained approach to advertising than is found in conventional media. Its effect has been marked. In the third quarter of 2009, advertising revenues earned by American newspapers dropped by 28% as compared with the corresponding period in 2008; revenues from the first nine months of 2009 also dropped by 29%. Clearly, a component of this decline is the credit crunch problems experienced by American firms in these years; however, it is an important part of a trend that has occurred since the early part of the decade.

The television industry has also suffered drops in income. For example, according to analysis carried out by *The Times*, Google earned £327 million in the United Kingdom compared with £317 million for all of the British commercial channel ITV1's output during the period between July and September 2007.

IT outsourcing

In 2011, my BT Internet connection failed; this was, for me, the equivalent of having my electricity or water cut off (something discussed in the final chapter of this book when I look at the work of Nicholas Carr). I rang the BT helpline and an Indian voice replied. Over the next 20 minutes, using the Internet, he took control of my computer. He opened folders, changed some settings, and restarted some programs, and, lo and behold, my connection restarted. I'm not often agog, but this time I was. I watched my mouse pointer travel over my screen guided by an invisible hand – I had the feeling I get when I drive past Heathrow airport and see a Boeing 747 taking off: a feeling of knowing that what I saw was possible, but not quite believing it. For the record, the fault was not BT's: I was in the habit of switching my Internet modem on and off and, during the off period, it had missed an important update.

This is an example of outsourcing. In a number of conventional industries, outsourcing has been the norm. For example, much of the clothing sold in the United Kingdom has been manufactured in countries such as China, India, and the Dominican Republic; and electronic devices are often made in low-labour-cost economics, for example my iPod is made in China. However, outsourcing is now common in systems development.

Pinsent Masons, one of the United Kingdom's leading law firms, have listed the arguments for using an external software developer: lower costs because of efficiencies and economies of scale; access to high-level IT skills (for example, software developers in India are some of the most accurate and sophisticated coders in the world and use advanced tools for systems development; they also have the largest proportion of companies certified to produce software of the highest reliability); removing non-core business from a company's infrastructure; minimizing large capital expenditure on IT infrastructure; and having some degree of certainty of future IT spend.

The Internet has provided an infrastructure that enables customers to talk to systems analysts in other countries via video links, send documents via emails, and test systems via live links. The result is that computer-based development is increasingly being moved offshore. For example, in 2006, the research company Computer Economics reported that 61% of all the American companies they surveyed outsourced some or all of their software development.

As I sit typing this chapter, three years after one of the greatest upheavals to our financial system, the future of IT outsourcing is unclear; on the one hand, companies are cutting back on IT investment, on the other hand, offshore outsourcing companies offer significant savings in investment. These two factors, together with increases in IT skills levels, will determine the growth of outsourcing over the next few decades.

The type of outsourcing I discuss above is thick-grained outsourcing in that you hire a company to carry out some set of IT functions. There is also a much thinner-grained version. There are now a number of web sites that provide details of software staff for hire (often these programmers are from Eastern Europe). So, if you have a project that requires a small amount of software development over a limited time, then video links and emails can put you in touch with developers who are competitive compared with Western European rates.

Citizen journalism

The term 'citizen journalism' is used to describe how ordinary citizens have become empowered by cheap computers and Internet connections to involve themselves in the reporting of reaction to events and publishing news articles and opinion articles. There are a number of technologies that are used for this: the main ones are blogs (online diaries), podcasts, video footage, digital photographs, and web sites.

There are a number of manifestations of this phenomenon. There are news blogs which aggregate news and contain comments not just by the blogger, but also by other Internet users who are able to insert comments at the end of the blog text. These blogs can be general in content or specific to a particular topic such as technology.

There are also news web sites which contain the same type of material that would be found in the web site of a conventional newspaper. Some of these sites take a neutral viewpoint; often, though, they report and comment on the news from a particular position, for example from the point of view of the Green movement.

Some of the most interesting manifestations of citizen journalism are participatory news sites where computer users post articles, other users tag the articles with descriptors that provide easy indexing, and, on some sites such as Digg, users vote on which articles are interesting. The articles with the greatest number of posts are then promoted to a prominent position on the web site.

One of the results of the drop in price of computers and silicon circuits has been the accompanying drop in price and availability of digital devices. One of the areas where this has been most marked is in digital recording. To my left, while I write this chapter, I have a digital recorder made by the Marantz company. It costs about £400, produces sound quality comparable to the recorders used by radio interviewers, and is a fraction of the cost and more convenient than the tape-based recorders of the preceding decade. Anyone can buy two condenser microphones, a cheap sound mixer, and one of these recorders for about £800, and can turn themselves into an Internet radio station. Many do.

The computer and the Internet have provided a medium for free expression that was only available to journalists up until the beginning of this decade. The most that anyone could have expected previously was a letter to the editor which might or might not have been selected. Now, as soon as there is a major story, the Internet is swamped by traffic.

An example of this effect happened in November 2009. A hacker successfully accessed a computer used by the Climatic Research Unit at the University of East Anglia. This is one of the foremost global warming research units in the world. Within days, there was a maelstrom of emails, audio podcasts, video podcasts, blog entries, and news stories circulating within the Internet. The director of the unit stepped down while an independent review looked into the claims.

Five days after it appeared, I did a search on Google using the word 'Climategate', the term used by climate sceptics to label the incident. There were over 13 million hits. I also checked on the video YouTube site, and there were over 16,000 hits when I typed in the same keyword.

It is clear that in one direct way (its ability to spread news) and one indirect way (its lack of security) the computer has had and will have a major effect on journalism.

Digital photography

For a long time I used film cameras. I would buy a film – usually containing enough space for 36 exposures – at the local chemist or photographer's, and load it into the camera, take the photographs, and then return the exposed film to the chemist for developing. The chemist would then send the film to a developing laboratory and, eventually, I would collect my 'snaps'. Hobbyists would sometimes develop their own photographs; for this, they needed to soak the film in a variety of chemicals and then take the negatives and place them in a device known as an enlarger. This would then produce an image on a sheet of paper soaked with chemicals. The paper would then be developed in a number of trays containing more chemicals. All this took place almost in the dark using just red light.

I now take photographs with a digital camera, and at the setting I use, I can take hundreds of photographs. All I need do to look at them is to load them into a computer and use one of a number of image viewer and manipulation programs that are available.

A hobbyist who wanted to modify a film-based image would have to carry out some complex, error-prone manipulations; for example, they would have to pass cardboard shapes between the beam of the enlarger and the photo in order to restrict the light and hence alter the light values of the image. Modern photograph-manipulation programs such as Photoshop provide facilities that enable the photographer to manipulate a photograph in a variety of ways, for example changing colours, changing exposure on the whole of a photograph or part of a photograph, tinting, creating effects similar to those achieved by post-Impressionist painters, and picking on areas in a photograph and enlarging them.

In 2002, the sales of digital cameras surpassed those of film cameras. Whenever I go to a tourist spot I now very rarely see a film camera in use. The trend since then has been for digital cameras to have better and better facilities, such as a greater resolution. This change is due to hardware improvements, faster processors, the increase in density of pixels in image sensors, and a reduction in circuit size. There has also been an increase in the facilities photographic software offers. For example, there is a technique known as High Dynamic Range imaging (HDR) that can be used to produce ultra-realistic photographs which are combined from a number of versions of a digital photo that are taken with different exposure values.

There has also been a trend for digital cameras to be embedded in other devices, primarily mobile phones. The growth of mobile phones has been staggering. In 2002, there were approximately 1 billion mobile subscriptions and one billion fixed-line subscriptions in the world. In 2008, there were approximately 1.27 billion fixed-line subscriptions and 4 billion mobile subscriptions. The vast majority of these phones in the Western world feature a camera. One effect of this is that it has created a citizen journalist movement. For example, Janis Krums produced the first photo of US Airways flight 1549 in the Hudson river after ditching because of engine problems. He took the picture on his iPhone minutes after the plane ditched in the water – a dramatic photograph showing passengers standing on one of the plane's wings while others huddled on the floating emergency chute. In June 2009, there were major protests in Iran about the alleged rigging of the presidential election; many of these protests were broken up violently by the authorities. Pictures showing this could be found on the Internet minutes later, as protestors sent photographs taken with their phones to friends outside Iran.

There are a number of other effects of the rise of digital photography. One obvious one is the demise of the chemical developing laboratories. The increasing power of computers and their increasing miniaturization has meant that such laboratories had no easy upgrade path to change themselves into digital laboratories, since the local photography shop or chain chemist can now invest in sophisticated digital photographic equipment – all that is left now are a few very specialist firms which cater for the fine art industry, for example photographers who take highly detailed black and white photographs.

There are some less obvious effects. A number of cultural commentators have raised the problem of trust in photographs. For example, political opponents circulated a digital photo of presidential candidate Senator John Kerry next to Jane Fonda at an anti-Vietnam war rally – the photo was doctored. There are a number of examples of institutions inserting faces of black people into photographs to give an impression that they are more raciably diverse.

All of this raises questions about which images we can trust. Clearly, this sort of manipulation could have been done with film technology, but it would be much less easy to do. To doctor a digital image using a computer program is far easier: it took me 4 minutes to transpose a picture taken of my wife in our village and add a background taken in Avignon to give the impression that she accompanied me on my trip.

Digital photography also has another citizen journalism effect over and above the use of the mobile phone. The Abu Ghraib incident arose from the sending of digital photographs of American soldiers mistreating Iraqi prisoners to friends and acquaintances.

The digital camera also provides more opportunities for creativity. Artists such as John Simon, Shawn Brixey, and Pascal Dombis routinely use the computer in their work. Dirck Halstead, a professor at the University of Texas, carried out a survey of the readers of the magazine *The Digital Journalist* that asked the readers about their attitudes to digital camera technology. All of them preferred digital technology; one surprising result from the survey was that the creativity that it offered was more of an advantage than factors such as speed and convenience.

Science and the computer

One of the startling things happening in science research is that it is being deluged with data. Computers are now routinely being used to store and analyse billions of items of data from satellites orbiting the earth, from land-based weather stations, and from large-scale nuclear experiments.

As an example of this, the Large Synoptic Survey Telescope, which is due to come into operation in the next ten years; it uses very sophisticated computer hardware, hardware similar to that used in digital photography, and will, in its first year of operation, produce something like 1.3 petabytes of data, more than any other telescope has provided by a very large margin.

This flood of data is providing scientists with major opportunities to analyse and predict, for example predicting the effect of high rainfalls on flooding near major centres of population. However, it is also providing some major problems. There are large numbers of diverse research groups throughout the world producing data. If a research group, say in atmospheric physics, wants the data and program code from another group, the normal process is to send an email, and if another group wants the same data, then the same process occurs. So the first problem that scientists are facing is that of distributed data.

The second problem is that there is no acceptable standard for storage. There are two components associated with the storage of data. First there is the data itself: large amounts of floating point numbers separated by symbols such as spaces or commas. Second, there is metadata. This is data that describes the raw data.
For example, if the data were from a series of temperature measuring stations throughout the globe the metadata would identify the part of the raw data that specified the station, the periods over which the data was sampled, and the accuracy of the data. Currently we have no standard way of specifying these two components.

The third problem is that it is not just data that are important in scientific enquiry. For example, when a physicist looks at data that are being used to prove or disprove global warming, they are analysed using computer programs, and embedded within these programs is code that carries out some statistical processes. It is very difficult to develop completely error-free computer programs. If other scientists want to audit their colleagues' work or progress it, then they will need access to program code.

The advent of the embedded computer – embedded in measuring instruments and observational instruments such as radio telescopes – has been disruptive to science. Clearly there is a need for much more attention to the archiving of data. There are some initiatives that address this such as the Australian National Data Service, but much more is needed.

The long tail

In 2007, Chris Anderson published the book *The Long Tail*. Anderson, a staffer at *Wired* magazine, pointed out that if you

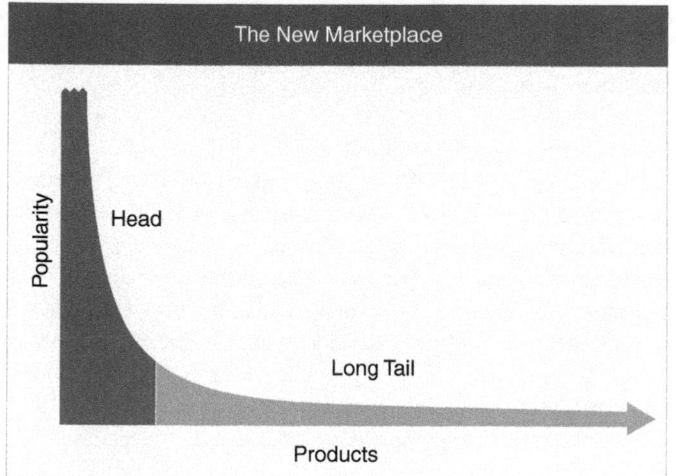

7. The long tail

looked at the sales of digital objects such as books you would see the graph shown as Figure 7. The horizontal axis shows books while the vertical axis shows sales. What you see is a standard curve for items that have a number of different instantiations, for example books, DVDs, and computer programs.

What the graph shows is that there is a comparatively small number of books that have large sales at the head of the graph and that there is a long tail of books that have small sales.

The key idea behind Anderson's thesis is that digitization promises the seller of digital items as much profit in selling the items in the tail as there is in selling items at the head. In the past, booksellers were hampered in what they sold by expensive stocking costs and the physical limitations of their shops. Publishers had similar constraints: every few years, I would receive a polite letter from one of my publishers informing me that one of my books is going out of print and would I like to buy some of the remaining stock.

Going out of print effectively means there will be no more copies available via conventional bookshops and nothing in the publisher's warehouse.

One of the key properties of digital objects is that you require very little space to store them: all that is required is a computer and some large disk storage to keep all the books that a major publisher prints. Anderson's thesis is that because of this there are major opportunities for sellers and publishers at the end of the long tail where the individual sales of esoteric books may be small, but the overall sales may match those of the bestsellers at the head of the tail.

Anderson's ideas have been challenged by a number of researchers who point out that his enthusiasm for the idea that revenues in the long tail are comparable with the head may not hold. However, what they miss is that digital technology may mean that esoteric titles such as *Steam Trains of Romania in the Early Part of the Twentieth Century*, or a DVD on early Japanese horror movies that feature zombies, might not match the sales of the latest bodice ripper, but they do offer, along with many other esoterica, opportunities for increased sales. For the major publisher and the book chain, the computer is disruptive in a positive way: for the specialist bookseller sourcing rare, non-antique works, the disruption is in the other direction.

Books and the e-reader

When I go for my lunch, I pass a colleague who has a small, flat, computer-based device in his hand. It's an e-reader. An e-reader allows him to download books from either a publisher's web site or a bookseller's site. I saw a prototype e-reader in 2005 and was not impressed, mainly because the quality of the screen was poor. My colleague's e-reader is vastly superior. The emergence of the e-reader reflects a trend that has happened in music whereby vinyl records gave way to CDs and where CDs are steadily giving way to sound files such as those that are played by the iPod. There is an interesting debate going on about the future of e-books and e-readers, the result of which will determine whether, in a decade or two, we will see the end of the conventional bookshop.

On the one hand there are those who point out that many people buy books for a quasi-aesthetic experience, that while reading is obviously the main purpose in buying a book, a well-produced art book, for example, with glossy pages and high definition, is an artefact that is pleasurable to handle and to look at. There are also those who point out that the price differential between online books and their printed version is not that large; this is due to the fact that most of the cost of a book comes from its marketing, its editing, the profit that a bookshop makes, and the profit that the publisher makes, and because of this small price differential there will be no major shift from printed media into electronic media.

However, there are those who compare the growth of e-books to the growth of music files who state that the same differentials hold between online music and CDs. They also point out that text is a static medium and that e-books that feature video and audio clips and links to web sites would provide a much richer reading experience – one that would drive readers towards e-books.

It is early days yet – however, the indications are that the growth of e-books is accelerating. A survey by the Association of American Publishers in conjunction with the International Digital Publishing Forum recently showed an exponential growth. For example, wholesale revenue from e-books in the third quarter of 2008 was 14 million dollars, while in the corresponding quarter of 2009, it was around 47 million dollars. I do not want to make a case that these figures show that in *n* years e-books will dominate; after all, the sales of conventional books greatly outweigh the sales of e-books. For example, the Association of American Publishers reported sales of 1.26 billion dollars for conventional books. However, the data shows the sort of trend that occurred with the increasing availability of sound files for devices such as the iPod.

In late 2009, *The Bookseller*, the trade magazine for British bookshops and publishers, released the results of a survey into the commercial possibilities of e-books. They were quite surprising: although 88% of the thousand-odd respondents stated that they felt that the e-reader was a threat to their business, many felt that there were commercial opportunities. One typical response was

> Everyone will gain by making reading easier and more accessible – and by widening the appeal to younger people (i.e. mobile audiences). High street book shops need to become service providers for readers – technology, some printed books (e.g. children's books, maps, art books), advice, author readings, seminars, learning centres, event hosts, etc.

One scenario is that the conventional chain bookshop disappears under pressure from online competition, but the local bookshop makes a comeback by becoming a venue and social centre and perhaps a micro-publisher.

My view is that it is not clear what will happen with respect to the balance between conventional book sales and the sales of e-books. However, here is one scenario. That there will be an increase in e-books that lie outside the considerable categories of fiction and non-fiction that have a personal viewpoint. For example, a prime area for e-books is encyclopaedias and dictionaries. The online project Wikipedia has already shown the way here: each entry not only contains text on a Wikipedia article, but also cross references other articles – often too much – and contains many cross-links to relevant items such as papers, news articles, and blogs.

Another area where e-books could take off is travel books where, as well as conventional text, the book would contain items such as video clips and photographs. As an experiment, I typed in the keywords 'Musee d'Orsay', a fantastic art gallery in Paris that has been converted from a railway station that holds some of the greatest 19th-century and 20th-century paintings. I got 47,000 hits. I looked at the first two hundred and, with a few exceptions, the quality of the photography is excellent and provides a good indication of the variety and importance of the holdings in one of my favourite art galleries. I also checked on the video hosting site YouTube and received 1,800 video clips.

Another area that could experience explosive growth is that of instruction manuals, for example cookbooks and car-maintenance manuals. Here, video clips showing some of the more tricky cooking techniques would be interspersed with conventional text and photographs.

There are many other categories of book that could be transformed by e-book technology. For example, school textbooks could contain video podcasts explaining a difficult point. However, at the end of the day, there is a huge edifice that e-books need to address: that of the novel and the non-fiction book which has a personal viewpoint, such as a single-writer history of the Second World War.

There are a number of factors that may accelerate the trend. The first is the availability of free material – open source text if you like. Project Gutenberg is a project that has a long history: it started in the early 1970s when its founder, Michael Hart, typed the Declaration of Independence into the mainframe computer at the University of Illinois. Since then volunteers have typed and digitized over 30,000 books into the Project Gutenberg web site. All the books are out of copyright and contain a high proportion of esoterica. However, there are many novels written by authors such as Dickens, Forster, and Scott Fitgerald which can be loaded into an e-reader – legally and for free.

A wild card that may affect the growth of novels and non-fiction work is Google. Over the last six years the company has been digitizing books on an industrial scale. This has been done in conjunction with libraries around the world such as those at

Columbia University and Cornell University. In 2009, the current count of Google digitized books stood at 10 million. Most of these books were available for partial search but around a million could be read in their entirety. The spread of Google books, the alacrity with which publishers now produce electronic versions of paper books and the technological advances that have produced a new generation of e-readers has created a major threat to paper books.

Another factor that may drive the cost of books down is that of online advertising. Every year I go to the Oxford Literary Festival – usually with my wife. Last year we attended a session in which two of my favourite authors were interviewed and fielded questions. They were Donna Leone, who writes crime novels based in Venice, and Kate Atkinson, who writes high-quality, uncategorizable novels. Before we attended their session, I predicted to my wife that the vast majority of the audience would be women and middle class. A quick head-count confirmed that about 95% were certainly women – I suspect that the same proportion were middle class. This congregation is a marketer's dream.

One of the key tools of marketers is targeting: knowing what the demographics are of the potential audience for some media item: a TV programme, a newspaper, or a TV channel. Most targeting is broad-based: the audience for Channel 4 in the United Kingdom has a number of broad traits as does the readership of *The Daily Telegraph* and you find advertising addressing these.

The purchasers of a book are a much better-focused target than, say, the readers of a particular newspaper. The purchaser of a book on the natural world may be interested in other books that are similar to the one bought (a trick that Amazon uses to display possible books to a visitor to their site), they may be interested in holidays which involve activities such as observing wild animals, or they may just need a new pair of binoculars.

The e-reader sold by Amazon already has Internet access built in, as has the iPad – a multi-function device developed by Apple. Soon all e-readers will have this capability. It raises the prospect that e-book prices could be driven downward for those who want to purchase a title that has advertising on part of the screen, where the cost of the books is reduced by advertising revenues.

Chapter 7
The cloud computer

Introduction

Whenever my wife or I visit out local Tesco supermarket we take part in an implicit contract: we buy our groceries and, before handing over our credit card, we give the checkout person our Tesco Clubcard. This card is swiped and the computer in the checkout till sends the card number and the items that we buy to a central computer. The use of such cards has revolutionized marketing. Previous to their use the information from a checkout computer was aggregated information, for example, how much of a certain product was bought in a week and whether there was an increased demand for a certain product at specific times of the year. By being able to associate a collection of purchases with a particular customer or family group of customers, a supermarket is able to carry out some very canny marketing.

Tesco will know that: my family buys lots of fresh food, that if it is a Wednesday we will buy some pre-cooked meals, and that red wine is the *drink du jour* of our house. I am relaxed about the data that is held: I gain an advantage because it enables Tesco to send me special offer vouchers for items that they think I would like and buy more frequently; it also adds to the Air Mile travel points that come with the Tesco Club Card; and Tesco get an advantage in knowing what my family spending habits are. It is a deal that I am not prepared to make with a pharmaceutical retailer since purchases there are associated with health.

Loyalty cards were the first manifestation of an explosion of data; an explosion that the Internet caused and which can be used by both companies and individuals with access to a browser. The aim of this chapter is to look at how the Internet has transformed the computer to the point where when you refer to the web as a massive computer you cannot be accused of science-fiction foolishness.

Open and closed data

The Tesco data are an example of closed data: the only people who can see it are marketers employed by that company. There is plenty of closed data that has been generated by users of the Internet. A good example is the data collected by the Amazon web site. Whenever I log in to that site I am greeted by a front page that displays books that Amazon thinks that I like. The books that are displayed are based on my past buying habits. For example, if I bought a book on contract bridge one week, then the web site will point me at other books on this card game.

Such closed data is valuable to large companies that make their money from selling or hiring items to the general public. A startling example of the lengths companies will go to improve the processing of this data is the Netflix Prize. Netflix is a company that rents out and streams videos to customers. It has a large database of customer preferences and tastes, and it was able to predict that if a customer selected a particular DVD, then there would be a good chance that they would want to borrow similar DVDs. The company used a computer program to make the predictions; however, it was felt that the program could be improved, and what Netflix did was to set a challenge to the programming community to come up with a better program. The prize for this was $1 million. In 2009, the prize was won by a team of programmers, the majority of whom worked for American and European systems companies.

As well as closed data, there is a huge quantity of open data that can be accessed by anyone who can use a browser. In 2000, the Canadian gold-mining firm Goldcorp placed its crown jewels on the Internet for everyone to see.

The company had hit bad times: its current holdings were looking mined out, the price of gold was falling, and the company lurched from crisis to crisis. Goldcorp's chief executive officer Rob McEwen decided to make the company's exploration data – its crown jewels – public and run a competition in which members of the public would process the data and suggest future exploration sites. Goldcorp offered $575,000 in prizes to the best entries.

It is not clear what the motives for McEwen's radical move were: desperation or an insight into how the power of crowds could be harnessed. Whatever the reason the competition was a huge success. A wide variety of people entered it: military men, academics, working geologists, retired geologists, and hobby geologists. The result was that new, very productive sites were found. The competition transformed Goldcorp into a major player in the gold exploration market and increased its value from $100 million to many billions of dollars.

The Goldcorp competition marked the start of an explosion in the availability of open data to the public; not only data that could be gained from processing public web pages, but data that would normally be hidden away in the computer networks of a commercial concern.

An example of public data is the online encyclopaedia Wikipedia. This has become one of the major successes of the Internet; it contains over 2.5 million entries all contributed by Internet users and is an example of the collaborative spirit that I will describe in this chapter. What is not generally known about Wikipedia is that it is a major resource for researchers and commercial developers who are concerned with natural language processing, for example companies producing programs that summarize thousands of words into an easily digestible form and scan the Internet for texts – newspaper articles, reports, magazine articles, and research papers – that deal with a particular topic.

One of the problems with natural language texts is that of ambiguity. The classical example of this, quoted in many textbooks on the subject, is the sentence

> They are flying planes.

This could have a number of meanings. It could refer to the pilots of commercial planes or pilots of planes flown by members of the armed forces. It could also be used by someone pointing at a number of planes in the sky. It could even be used to describe children flying model planes.

By itself, this sentence is difficult to understand. However, what makes it understandable is its context. For example, if it occurs in an RAF recruitment brochure, then it would have the first meaning. Researchers have found that Wikipedia provides a very useful resource for tasks such as understanding text. In order to understand this, look at the extract below from the encyclopaedia.

> Public cloud or external cloud describes cloud computing in the traditional mainstream sense, whereby resources are dynamically provisioned on a fine-grained, self-service basis over the Internet, via web applications/web services, from an off-site third-party provider who shares resources and bills on a fine-grained utility computing basis.

The extract comes from an entry on cloud computing which underlies much of this chapter. The underlined terms within the extract are references to other Wikipedia entries. It is these which provide a context for understanding a sentence. For example, if a sentence in an article contains the word 'cloud' and many of the cross references in the Wikipedia article on cloud computing occur in the article you would be able to identify it as one about a particular brand of computing rather than meteorology.

Another example of open data is that generated by Twitter. This is a technology that allows its users to deposit short messages on a web site that others can read; it's a bit like the messaging you get with mobile phones, the only difference being the fact that the messages (tweets) are public.

Tweets are being used by the US Geological Survey (USGS) to get public reaction to earthquakes. They provide a near instant feedback as to the severity of a tremor and enable emergency services to be organized a little more quickly than they would be via conventional monitoring.

The USGS continuously collects geo-codes (these are identification codes supplied by mobile devices such as 3-G mobile phones) and stores the tweets associated with the codes. When the US national seismic network detects an earthquake, a system then checks to see if there was a significant increase in messages following the event and the nature of the messages. Staff can then examine the messages to see what the effect of the earthquake was.

APIs

So, I have given you examples of databases that can be manipulated by a computer for a number of purposes. The important question is: how is this data made available? The key is something known as an Application Programming Interface (normally abbreviated to API).

An API is a collection of software facilities that allow you to access Internet-based resources. For instance, Amazon has an API that allows programmers to query data about the products that Amazon sells. For example, you can retrieve the unique ISBN of a book, and other product data that can be used for commercial activities. This might seem an innocuous thing to do but, later in the chapter, I will describe how revolutionary this is.

There is a web site known as programmableweb.com which contains details of all the available APIs that can be used to access web resources. At the time of writing this chapter, there were just over 1,900 APIs listed.

So, what can you do with such facilities? A good example is that of someone setting themselves up as a specialist bookseller, for example selling books on France. Amazon has an associate program that provides facilities for anyone to advertise books stocked by the company on their own web site. Such a web site would contain links to the book entries on the Amazon web site and when a visitor to, say, the France book site clicks one of these links and buys the book Amazon pays the owner of the site a commission.

A good quality site with, for example, articles on France, recipes for French food, and latest news items, would draw visitors who would feel inclined to support the site by buying their books using the site links – after all, the price of the book would be the same as that displayed on the Amazon web site. The details on the web site about each book would be obtained using an API that is freely provided by Amazon.

This form of associate program – sometimes known as an affiliate program – is now very popular. The web site associateprograms.com lists many thousands of such programmes. It includes organizations in the media sector, the food sector, and the sport and recreation sector.

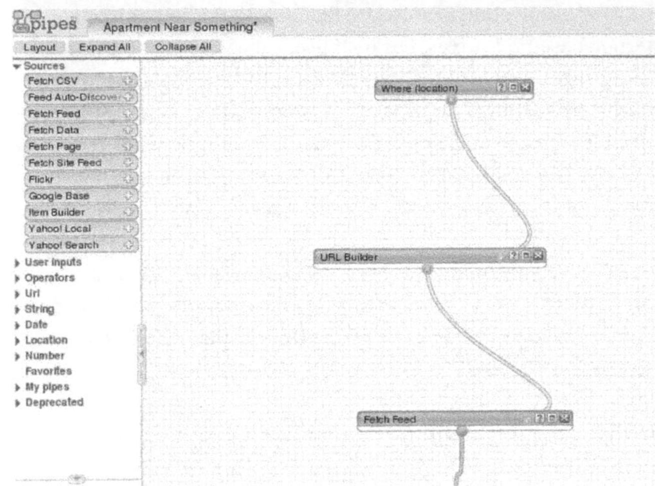

8. A Yahoo Pipes program

Another use of APIs is via something known as a mashup. The term 'mashup' comes from brewing where it is used to describe the bringing together of the ingredients for an alcoholic drink – usually beer. In computer terms, a mashup is the use of a number of APIs to create a hybrid application.

One of the first mashups was developed by the software developer Paul Rademacher. Google has stored a series of maps which can be viewed by anyone and for which it developed an API. Rademacher developed a program that took housing ads on the popular web site Craigslist and then displayed the location of the apartments or houses for sale on the maps published by Google.

There are many other examples. The web site programmableweb.com lists many thousands of examples with over half involving mapping. For example, it lists: a mashup which provides tourist guides for ten large American cities linked to videos on the YouTube site showing landmarks and visitor attractions, a mashup which allows visitors to share their most cherished books, and mashups of the location of crimes committed in American cities linked to the geographical location where they occurred.

Developing a mashup used to be something that was confined to software developers. However, the company Yahoo has developed a technology that enables anyone to develop mashups. The technology, known as Yahoo Pipes, is based on a very simple graphical programming language. It manipulates data feeds from web sites in order to create new applications.

Figure 8 shows an example of part of a Pipes program. To develop a Pipes program, all you have to do is to connect together a variety of boxes that carry out functions such as filtering data, recognizing data as important, passing it on to other boxes, and displaying data on a web page. While developing Pipes programs is not trivial, it is very much easier than many mashup techniques, and has lowered the technical barriers for anyone who wants to develop web-based applications.

Computers in the cloud

A number of the trends described in this chapter and in Chapter 1 point towards a vision of computing in the next decade as being highly centralized, with many of the functions carried out by computers such as the humble PC being transferred to a massive collection of server computers that reside in a virtual cloud. The last two years has seen an increase in facilities that reside in the cloud.

In the 1990s, if you wanted to use a software package, say an HR package which managed the staff in your company, then you would buy such a package and install it on the computers owned by your company. The package would normally be sent to you on some magnetic medium such as a CD or a DVD and technical staff in your company would then install it on any computers that needed it. Technical staff would then look after the software: installing new versions, tuning it for optimum performance, and answering any technical queries from users.

The increased speed of Internet access has meant that a different business model is emerging. Here the users of a package would not access it on their own computers, but use an Internet connection to access the software, with the software residing on a computer operated by the package developer. There would be a number of advantages in doing this.

The first advantage is that it would require less technical staff, or at least enable staff to concentrate on other tasks rather than spending time being trained and keeping up-to-date on the arcane knowledge required to maintain the package.

The second advantage is that it reduces the effort required to maintain versions of the software. Large software systems are often updated, for example when enough customers require new functions or when a law is changed that requires a company to behave differently. The process of installing an update can be something of a technical nightmare for staff who don't have the technical skills. By having only one copy of the software resident at a single computer, the update process is much more straightforward.

A third advantage is that computer hardware costs are reduced. The cloud computing concept envisages both the software and the data it requires reside in the cloud. Theoretically all that would be needed for a company to access a package in the cloud would be a very cut-down computer with little, if any, file storage – effectively what was known as a 'dumb terminal' in the 1970s.

The proponents of cloud computing claim that: it enables companies to be a lot more agile in their business, reduces both human and hardware costs, enables users to connect anywhere to software rather than just from a computer that resides in their office environment, enables a much higher hardware efficiency as a server on which a package resides can use up the slack resources I detailed in Chapter 1 more effectively, enables a more efficient use of resources, and addresses the green agenda. It also enables a higher degree of security because all the data that are used are held on a limited number of servers rather than being scattered around a large number of individual personal computers which are prone to both technical security attacks and attacks which arise from physical security problems.

There are also potential problems with cloud computing. First, what happens when a company becomes bankrupt? If no company is keen to take over the bankrupt company, it would severely embarrass the customers of the defunct company. Second, although there is an argument that security is enhanced when cloud computing is employed, there is the problem that if a security violation occurred at the cloud company's installation, then the effect would be much larger. If a single company had its data stolen, then that's a major problem for the company: if the data were stolen from a cloud company, *all* its customers would be compromised.

Cloud computing is not just confined to industrial and commercial packages, it is beginning to affect the home computer user. A good example of this is email. Many computer users have switched to smartphone-based email programs and to web-based mail systems. One example of this is Google Apps. This is a set of office-based tools which include a word processor, an email program, and a calendar. If you are happy with basic features, then these applications are free. Not only are the applications free, but also the storage that you use is free, for example the storage for word-processed documents.

One of the most interesting writers on the evolution of computing is Nicholas Carr. He has written two books which have divided the

IT community. The first is *Does IT Matter*. Here he argued that the strategic importance of information technology in business has diminished as information technology has become more commonplace, standardized, and cheaper. In this and a number of more academic articles, he pointed out in 2004 that as hardware costs decline, companies would purchase their computing almost as if it was a utility such as electricity and gas. Cloud computing is an example of this.

His second book, *The Big Switch: Rewiring the World, from 'Edison' to 'Google'*, takes the theme of utility computing further and uses the analogy of the growth of the electricity industry to shine a light on what is starting to happen in computing. Carr points out that the electricity generation industry started out almost as a cottage industry. A company that needed electrical power would install its own generator and have it maintained by its engineering staff; something which gave rise to a major demand for engineers with heavy electrical engineering skills. He shows that pioneers such as Edison changed the world of electrical generation to the point where electricity was generated and distributed by major utility companies.

In a series of elegant analogies, Carr shows the same forces at work in computing: where gradually services are migrating to large collections of servers that reside on the Internet rather than in some company premises. The implications of this, which I shall explore in the final chapter, include: a shift of control from media and other institutions to individuals, major worries about security and privacy, and the export of the jobs of highly skilled knowledge workers.

The social computer

In 1995, a web site was placed on the Internet. This site, known as WikiWikiWeb, has transformed the way we use computers. It was developed in order to help programmers in software engineering communicate with each other – effectively, it was the electronic version of the white board. Engineers could add ideas to the white board, delete anything they thought was irrelevant, and modify the thoughts of others.

Up until this site went live, traffic from computers to the Internet was mainly one way. If you wanted to view a web page, then you would click on a link, a short message of a few bytes would be sent to a web server, and a page containing thousands of bytes would be returned and displayed on your browser. WikiWikiWeb started a process whereby the interaction between a computer user and the Internet became much more two-way.

There were some early examples of two-way communication. For example, the online bookseller Amazon invited users of its web site to post comments on the books that they read. These comments were then inserted into the web page that contained details of the book. However, this interaction was not instantaneous: it was intercepted by a human editor for checking and then inserted.

The inventor of WikiWikiWeb was Ward Cunningham, a researcher and consultant. He wanted to be able to communicate with fellow workers in such a way that they could use a virtual white board. Cunningham's idea has spawned a software system known as a 'wiki'. What a wiki does is to maintain a document or series of documents within the Internet. Users of the wiki are then allowed to modify its contents – even being allowed to delete some content. Most inventions associated with the computer can be seen as being prompted by some improvement in software or hardware. The invention of the wiki was unusual as it was conceptually simple and required very little change to existing systems.

Arguably the best example of a wiki is Wikipedia. This online encyclopaedia has been developed by thousands of volunteers;

a controversial study carried out by the prestigious science journal *Nature* compared it with the equally prestigious *Encyclopædia Britannica* and came to the conclusion that they were close in terms of accuracy.

There are many applications of wikis. For example, companies use them for interacting with customers: eliciting views about current products and services and discovering what customers want. Another example is the use of a wiki for running large projects – particularly those that are split across a number of geographic locations. My own university – a university where the vast majority of students study at home – uses wikis to enable students to collaborate with each other; it provides a virtual form of interaction similar to the social interaction that would occur in a conventional university.

Wikis heralded an era of two-way communication that is now the norm on the Internet. The social networking site Facebook is a good example of this. Facebook is a site that allows anyone to join, set up their own personal pages, and communicate with groups of other Internet users who are known as 'friends'. One of the many facilities offered by Facebook is 'the wall'. This is a shared area where a user and their friends can write messages that they can all access and read.

Wikis are just one component in the increasing use of the computer for social communication and in the development of collaborative products. Twitter is a web site that allows very short messages (known as 'tweets') to be sent from anyone with a connection to the Internet – mobile or otherwise. The web site Flickr allows users to store photographs on the web in such a way that anyone with a computer and a connection can look at and comment on them. YouTube is a video-sharing site that allows users to post short videos on the Internet and, like Flickr, allows anyone to comment on them; delicious is a web site that allows computer users to share the bookmarks of favourite web sites. Digg is a web site that enables users to share links and stories from anywhere in the world. Users of Digg can then vote on the stories and they will be elevated to a more prominent position on the site (a process known as 'digging') or reduced in prominence (a process known as 'burying').

The collaborative development of products is also an area that has blossomed over the last ten years. Wikipedia is, yet again, a good example of this: the development of a hugely comprehensive encyclopaedia by a large number of volunteers. There are, however, a number of other examples.

One academic example is OpenWetWare. This is an MIT project that aims to share knowledge in biology and which, via a number of collaborating institutions, stores research outputs such as articles and experimental protocols.

The computer as a data-mining tool

One of the consequences of the connections between the computer and the Internet and advances in storage technology is the large amount of data that is generated, stored, and made readily accessible to computer users. In general, the larger the amount of data that is stored the more information you can get out of it – but often at a higher processing cost.

A recent example of data-mining is described in Steven Levitt and Stephen Dubner's recent book *Superfreakonomics*. They describe how the financial records and habits of potential terrorists can be mined for information; this includes negative as well as positive features, an example of a negative feature being they were unlikely to have a savings account and a positive feature being the fact that there was no monthly consistency in the timing of their deposits or withdrawals.

One of the most graphic examples of large-scale data use is a recent advance in the computer translation of languages. Using a computer to translate between one language and another has been an aim of researchers since the 1960s. The normal approach to translate from a language *A* into a language *B* has been to devise a set of rules which describe the sentence structure of language *A*, process the text in language *A* that needs to be translated, discern its structure using the rules, and then using the rules of sentence structure of language *B* transform the text into its equivalent in that language.

Progress in what is known as 'machine translation' has been steady but slow. However, recent work at Google has accelerated the process. Researchers at the company have developed a new technique which relies on the use of a huge corpus of existing text. The researchers used a technique known as 'machine learning' to carry out the translation. Machine learning is a means by which a computer program is given a large number of cases and results and tries to infer some hypothesis from the data presented. In the Google case, the machine-learning program was presented with 200 billion words of text and their equivalents in other languages that were supplied by the United Nations; it then learned the way in which individual sentences were rendered from one language to another, without having any knowledge of the structure of any of the languages used. The next few years hold out the promise of improvement compared with programs that use rule descriptions of a language.

In his book *Planet Google*, Randall Stross describes how an Arabic sentence was transformed by a commercial translation system into 'Alpine white new presence tape registered for coffee confirms Laden', when the Google system translated it almost perfectly into 'The White House confirmed the existence of a new Bin Laden tape'.

At the start of this chapter, I described how loyalty cards provide useful information to retailers such as Tesco. This is an example of developing a database that can be used for a variety of marketing purposes and employing a computer to process it. There are many more. One major application of data-mining is market-basket analysis. Here, a company will keep past purchases and other data such as demographic information in order to improve its sales. For example, Amazon uses past sales to notify customers of items that they may find interesting and which are somehow associated with their past sales; for example, a customer who buys crime novels will almost invariably be presented with newly published crime fiction when they log on to the Amazon web site again.

Another example of the use of market-basket analysis is that of identifying what are known as 'alpha customers'. These are customers who have a career that places them in front of a large number of people. They may be celebrities who are often seen on television, and whose images are found in newspapers, or they may be business leaders who will be listened to in seminars and shareholder meetings. What is important is that these are people whose lifestyles are often copied or their advice taken.

Such an application of data-mining is only made profitable by a concept known as viral marketing whereby social sites such as Facebook amplify conversations between consumers and spread these conversations. There are a number of examples of how successful this can be. The film *The Blair Witch Project* would, in pre-Internet days, have become not just a cult film but a minor cult film; electronic word of mouth made it hugely successful.

One interesting commercial use of the technique of aggregating data is that of the prediction market. This is similar in many ways to a stock market where investors buy and sell shares in companies. However, in a prediction market it is a prediction: it might be a prediction about who will win an Oscar, what the election majority of a political party will be, or economic events such as a major change in a currency rate. When such markets are popular they can predict to a high degree of accuracy.
For example, a market that involved the buying and selling of

Oscar predictions correctly predicted 32 of the 36 big category nominees for the 2006 Oscars, and 7 out of the 8 top category winners.

From an Internet phenomenon prediction markets have now become something major companies use for economic prediction. For example, companies such as Google use internal prediction markets to determine business policy.

At the beginning of this book, I defined the computer as:

> A computer contains one or more processors which operate on data. The processor(s) are connected to data storage. The intentions of a human operator are conveyed to the computer via a number of input devices. The result of any computation carried out by the processor(s) will be shown on a number of display devices.

You may have thought that this was the academic in me coming out: relying on a definition, tying up loose ends, and attempting to be semantically clear. However, the point this definition makes is that it covers not only the computer on your desk that you use for tasks such as word-processing and web browsing, the computers that help fly a plane, or the computer chip embedded in an iPod, but also a much larger computer made up of hundreds of millions of computers and which is embedded in a cloud; I hope that this chapter has convinced you of this.

Chapter 8
The next computer

Introduction

The basic architecture of the computer has remained unchanged for six decades since IBM developed the first mainframe computers. It consists of a processor that reads software instructions one by one and executes them. Each instruction will result in data being processed, for example by being added together; and data being stored in the main memory of the computer or being stored on some file-storage medium; or being sent to the Internet or to another computer. This is what is known as the von Neumann architecture; it was named after John von Neumann, a naturalized American mathematician who was at the forefront of computer research in the 1940s and 1950s. His key idea, which still holds sway today, is that in a computer the data and the program are both stored in the computer's memory in the same address space.

There have been few challenges to the von Neumann architecture. In this final chapter, I shall look at two future approaches to computing which involve totally different architectures. I shall also look at a sub-architecture which is known as the 'neural net architecture', which has some resemblance to the neural structures in the brain. But, first, a strange piece of history which may repeat itself.

Functional programming and non-standard architectures

In the 1980s, there was a huge increase of research funding for computing researchers – undreamt of funds became available from British, European, and American sources. It would be nice to think that this occurred because of governments realizing the potential of computers. However, it occurred because of fear: fear of Japanese industries. The Japanese ministry of trade, MITI, had announced a major programme of funding into computer technology and Western governments, having experienced the havoc that the Japanese electronics and motor industries had caused, feared similar things might happen to their still-evolving computer industries.

The United Kingdom set up the Alvey programme. This was a joint programme between government departments and the Science Research Council, to advance both research and the supply of trained IT staff. There were a number of strands to this research, one of which was novel computer architectures.

In the 1980s, a number of researchers had described problems with software development and with the von Neumann architecture. Some pointed out that software developed with conventional programming languages was often error-ridden and that the painstaking process of instructing the computer to read data, process it, and write to memory was too detailed and complex. Other researchers pointed out that in the coming decades, hardware technology would advance to the point where large numbers of processors could be embedded on a single chip: that this offered major opportunities in terms of computing power, but would create more errors as programmers tried to share work amongst the processors.

In order to address these problems, computer scientists started developing a new class of programming languages known as

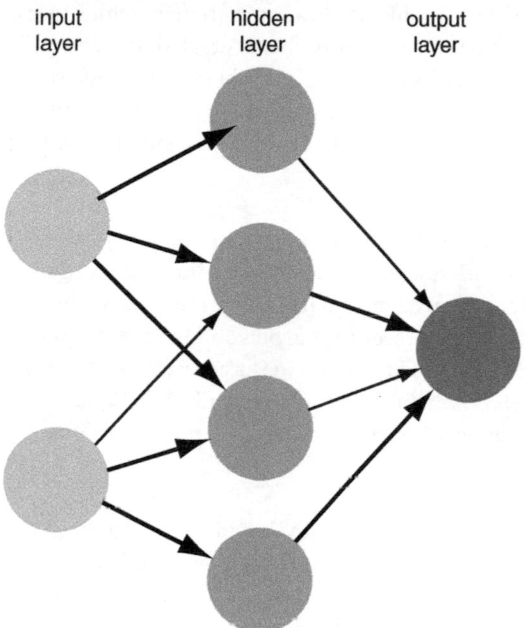

9. A simple neural network

'functional languages'. These languages did not have the step-by-step feature of a conventional programming language; rather, they consisted of a series of mathematical equations that defined the end result of the computation. It was left to the computer to 'solve' these equations and deliver the correct result.

A number of functional languages were developed: the four best-known are FP, Haskell, ML, and Miranda. A number of computer packages were also developed to execute programs in these languages. Unfortunately, there was a problem: the programs resided on von Neumann computers; this resulted in very slow execution times – conventional architectures were just not up to the job.

Because of the problems with conventional architectures, a number of research establishments created novel computers out of arrays of hardware processors. These processors would take a functional program and process an internal representation of the program, reducing it to a form that could be efficiently executed.

The results from this were not promising, and functional programming research and novel architectures declined as computer scientists moved into other areas such as grid computing. Until recently, the only remnant of this interesting research area could be found in the curriculum of computer science degrees where, very occasionally, functional programming is an element in first-year undergraduate teaching.

I used the words 'until recently' because there has been a resurgence of interest in functional languages. This has arisen because of the increasing availability of multi-processor chips and major increases in their speed. For example, in 2009, Intel announced a processor, the Single-chip Cloud Computer, that had 48 processors on a piece of silicon no bigger than a postage stamp. It has meant that, for example, publishers who are mainly associated with professional sales rather than academic sales have been releasing books on functional programming languages. As desktop computers become more powerful and include more processors, such languages should achieve much greater penetration, even if they are implemented on conventional architectures.

An interesting architecture that has applications over a relatively limited domain is the neural network. It is an architecture that has often been simulated on a von Neumann computer. It is used for pattern-recognition applications and for predicting short-term trends.

A cancer cell detection system based on neural nets was developed by Andrea Dawson of the University of Rochester Medical Center, Richard Austin of the University of California at San Francisco, and David Weinberg of the Brigham and Women's Hospital; this system can detect cancerous cells with an accuracy comparable to human detection.

Researchers at Queen Mary College, part of the University of London, have used neural networks in a security application where they are used to focus on the face of a possible intruder in a building even though the intruder may be moving.

Researchers at the University of Sussex have used the genetic programming idea that I described in Chapter 4 to create a number of generations of neural computers and select the best neural computer that solves problems in the area of pursuit and evasion where someone or something is trying to avoid a pursuer.

So, what is a neural computer, often called a 'neural network'? Initially, the idea of such a computer arose from studies of the neural architecture of the brain. Figure 9 shows a simple schematic. It consists of an input layer that can sense various signals from some environment, for example the pixels that make up a picture of a human face. In the middle (hidden layer), there are a large number of processing elements (neurones) which are arranged into sub-layers. Finally, there is an output layer which provides a result, for example this might be a simple window on a security system when, say, an airline passenger who is a potential terrorist is recognized.

It is in the middle layer that the work is done in a neural computer. What happens is that the network is trained by giving it examples of the trend or item that is to be recognized. What the training does is to strengthen or weaken the connections between the processing elements in the middle layer until, when combined, they produce a strong signal when a new case is presented to them that matches the previously trained examples and a weak signal when an item that does not match the examples is encountered.

Neural networks have been implemented in hardware, but most of the implementations have been via software where the middle layer has been implemented in chunks of code that carry out the learning process.

Before looking at other novel architectures, it is worth saying that although the initial impetus was to use ideas in neurobiology to develop neural architectures based on a consideration of processes in the brain, there is little resemblance between the internal data and software now used in commercial implementations and the human brain.

Quantum computers

In Chapter 4, I discussed how VLSI technology has enabled computer companies to develop more and more powerful computers; the increase in power arising from an increased ability to squeeze more and more processors on a single chip.

The von Neumann computer is based on the storage of data using binary digits (0 or 1) collected together into bytes. Quantum computers store data as quantum bits, or qubits; these can be implemented as atoms, ions, photons, or electrons. These qubits can not only act as a storage element for data but can also be combined together to implement a hardware processor.

In order to get an idea of how powerful a quantum computer can be, David Deutsch, an Oxford academic and physicist, and one of the pioneers in the area, has calculated that a modest 30-qubit computer could work at 10 teraflops. This is comparable to the speeds achieved by the supercomputers that were working in the first decade of this millennium.

One of the problems with using quantum ideas to implement a computer is concerned with the effect that observation of qubits could have. For example, trying to examine the state of a qubit could change its state along with others. This means that it could be immensely difficult to read data from a quantum computer – a process that is very easy with a conventional computer.

Happily, there is a quantum phenomenon known as entanglement which has come to the aid of the quantum computer developer. In 2006, physicists at the USA Commerce Department's National Institute of Standards and Technology reported in the 19 October edition of the science journal *Nature* that they had taken a major step towards moulding entanglement into a technique that can be used to read quantum-based data. They demonstrated a method for refining entangled atom pairs – a process called purification – which involved entangling two pairs of beryllium ions. This means that the data in a quantum computer can be observed indirectly without affecting its value.

Quantum computing is in its very early days. Results have been very small-scale so far: for example, a Canadian startup company, D-Wave, has demonstrated a working 16-qubit quantum computer. The computer solved a simple Sudoku puzzle and other pattern-matching problems. Now, compared with the performance of a conventional computer, this solution of a modestly sized problem is no huge achievement in terms of capability. However, it is a dramatic proof of concept.

Quantum computers are important in that a successful computer based on quantum physics ideas could overturn many of the technologies that are currently extant. One of the areas where it would have the most effect is in cryptography. A number of modern cryptographic methods rely on the fact that it is exceptionally hard to solve certain problems – problems that are known as wicked problems – however, researchers have pointed out that a relatively modest quantum computer *could* solve these problems; indeed, one of the challenges that this community have addressed is of doing just that.

For example, in 2001 computer scientists from IBM and Stanford University demonstrated that a quantum computer can be programmed to find the prime factors of numbers (a prime factor is a number which divides exactly into a number and which cannot be reduced further; for example, the prime factors of 33 are 3 and 11). The researchers employed a 7-qubit computer to find the factors of 15 (5 and 3). Prime factor determination is one of the problems that enable Internet-based cryptography to be successful.

Again, in computation terms this is no great achievement; in 2005, for example, researchers at the German Federal Agency for Information Technology Security used a cluster of conventional computers to factor a 200-digit number. However, it represents an important proof of concept which, if made industrial, would threaten a large segment of the technologies we use to send secure data.

The DNA computer

Deoxyribonucleic acid (DNA) is a nucleic acid that contains the genetic instructions used to determine the development and life of living organisms and some viruses. When biologists refer to DNA, they often talk about it in terms of a computer program: a program that, when executed, controls our physical growth and that makes up our genetic profile.

DNA contains data that consists of two long polymers of simple units called nucleotides. Within the DNA there are also sugars and phosphates. Attached to each sugar is one of four categories (A, T, C, and G) of molecules that are known as bases. These are the basic units that encode the information used in our genetic development.

Thus, we have a potential computer containing data and a program that manipulates this data. As early as 1994, the American computer scientist Leonard Adelman showed that a computer based on DNA could solve a problem known as the directed Hamiltonian path problem. This is a special version of the travelling salesman problem that was described in Chapter 4. The number of data points that were processed by Adelman's program were small: a desktop computer could have obtained the correct solution in a short amount of time. However, it represented a proof of concept.

These are the steps that this DNA computer might carry out in order to solve a problem: the strands of DNA would be regarded as the data for the problem. These would be codified using the A, T, C, and G encoding found in the bases.

These molecules would then be mixed, and a number of these DNA strands would stick together. Each collection of strands would represent a possible solution to the problem. Invalid answers would be removed by a series of chemical reactions. What would be left would be one or more solutions to the problem being solved.

After Adelman's epoch-making work, a number of research groups, alerted to the potential of using human genetic material, started looking at analogues between DNA and the von Neumann computer. Researchers at the University of Rochester have developed electronic circuits known as 'logic gates' out of genetic material. As you may remember from Chapter 1, a logic gate is an electronic device that takes a number of bits and produces as an output another binary bit that depends on the inputs. For example, And logic gates produce a 1 when their two inputs are 1 and a zero otherwise. In the same way that the components of DNA are the fundamental building blocks of life, the gates are the fundamental building blocks of computers; for example, they are used to implement arithmetic functions such as addition and subtraction.

DNA computers are clearly a radical departure from current computers in that the material used to produce them is of a chemical nature – current computers are made out of metal and silicon. However, they do not depart from the von Neumann idea, as the quantum computer does. What they do offer is a computation paradigm that offers massive amounts of storage and very little power dissipation. Like the quantum computer, they are only just emerging from the proof of concept stage.

A view from dystopia

Jonathan Zittrain is a distinguished Professor of Internet Governance. He has written a key work on the future of the Internet – not the technical future, but a future that could be constrained by government and industrial actions. It might seem odd to finish this book with a chapter that represents a somewhat dystopic view of the computer; after all, this entire book has been about the computer and has concentrated on the staggering advances it has made – so why finish with the Internet, and why finish on a downbeat note? The first question is easy to answer: this book has continually stressed that you cannot disengage the computer from the networked environment within which it now operates. The answer to the second question is that it is too easy to get carried away with the gee-whizzery of computing without considering some of the down points. I have done this a little in Chapter 3, where I briefly explored some issues of security and privacy.

The idea that the computer can solve major problems without, for example, looking at context, is an idea that still seems to have a great deal of currency. An example of this is the wastage that is associated with British government IT projects; large projects, such as the National Health IT project, have leaked money over the last decade. For example, a recent report by the Taxpayers' Alliance documented a large number of government projects that had reported budget overruns. It detailed overruns of around £19 billion, of which IT-based projects contributed £12 billion.

In the first part of his book, Zittrain describes the history of the computer. It starts at the point when individual computers were maintained by a professional class and when software systems satisfied narrow requirements, for example to produce the wage and salary slips of employees – this occurred around the 1960s. He then describes the processes whereby the PC gradually became part of many people's electronic furniture so that the non-technical user could install whatever software they wished, to the point when, via the Internet, it became a tool for mass creativity and mass collaboration.

In his book, Zittrain looks at the tensions between aspects of this metamorphosis: declining security, as detailed in Chapter 3, declining privacy as detailed in Chapter 5, and the notions of the computer and the Internet as a public property capable of informing, enabling collaboration, and encouraging creativity.

Zittrain describes a number of possible brakes on the development of the computer in terms of what it might be possible to do with it in the future. One potential brake is that of devices that allow access to the Internet, only in a way controlled by the manufacturers of the device. These devices include game consoles, MP3 players, digital TV recorders, and e-readers.

Such devices are either completely closed or almost fully closed and users are only allowed access and modification of the underlying software under strict conditions – usually such users develop third-party software for the device and are allowed access only after some commercial agreement is made.

A possible future implied by Zittrain is of an Internet in which access is via home computer terminals with little of the hardware power of the current PCs – they would just connect to the Internet – and where a host of tethered devices restrict the user in the same way that, for example, the North Korean government restricts external wireless reception in their country.

Zittrain's theme was preceded by ideas propanded by Nicholas Carr in his book *The Big Switch*. Carr's focus is commercial. In the book, he compares the growth of the Internet to the growth of electrical power generation. In the latter part of the 19th century and early part of the last century, power generation was carried out almost as a cottage industry, with each company maintaining its own generator and employing heavy electrical engineers to maintain them. Carr's book shows how Thomas Edison and Samuel Insull revolutionized the electricity-generation industry by developing an infrastructure whereby, initially, domestic consumers and then industrial consumers took their power from a grid. The move to electricity was rapid and was the result of advances in power generation and the radical step of replacing direct current power with alternating current power.

Carr compares this growth of electricity generation with the growth of the Internet. As you will have seen in Chapter 7, there is an increasing trend for computer power to be centralized. For example, there is an increasing number of sites that store your data securely; the grid allows the Internet to take the processing strain away from the PC; and, increasingly, companies are offering software functionality via a web site rather than by providing a facility where software can be installed on a PC or a server.

The infrastructure is already there for the replacement of the PC by cut-down, computer-based consumer devices that feature a screen, a keyboard, and enough hardware to allow the user to communicate with the Internet together with unmodifiable software embedded in firmware.

Carr's thesis is also supported by another writer, Tim Wu. In his book *The Master Switch*, Wu also takes a historical perspective which is based on the growth of television and other communication media. He points out that those technologies that were once free and open have eventually become centralized and closed as a result of commercial pressures.

So, another image of the computer of the future is as an embedded device within a piece of consumer electronics that interacts with the Internet via a browser; in which activities such as developing a piece of text would be carried out using a word processor held on a remote server. It would be a piece of electronics that prevents the user from modifying the device via software. In a few decades time, we may look at the desktop or laptop we currently use in the same way we look at photographs of early electricity-generation hardware.

Further reading

In this section, I have included a list of excellent books that are relevant to each chapter and which expand upon the main points made in each. Some of these are relevant to more than one chapter, so you will find some duplication.

The naked computer

M. Hally, *Electronic Brains: Stories from the Dawn of the Computer Age* (Granta Books, 2006).

C. Petzold, *Code: the Hidden Language* (Microsoft Press, 2000).

The small computer

C. Maxfield, *BeBOP to the Boolean Boogie: An Unconventional Guide to Electronics* (Newnes, 2008).

The ubiquitous computer

N. Christakis and J. Fowler, *Connected* (HarperCollins, 2011).

A. Greenfield, *Everyware: The Dawning Age of Ubiquitous Computing* (Peachpit Press, 2006).

J. Krumm (ed.), *Ubiquitous Computing Fundamentals* (Chapman and Hall, 2009).

K. O'Hara and N. Shadbolt, *The Spy in the Coffee Machine* (Oneworld Publications, 2008).

The global computer

C. J. Murray, *The Supermen: The Story of Seymour Cray and the Technical Wizards Behind the Supercomputer* (Wiley, 1997).

J. Naughton, *A Brief History of the Future: Origins of the Internet* (Phoenix, 2000).

M. M. Waldrop, *The Dream Machine: J. C. R. Licklider and the Revolution That Made Computing Personal* (Penguin Books, 2002).

J. Zittrain, *The Future of the Internet* (Penguin Books, 2009).

The insecure computer

K. O'Hara and N. Shadbolt, *The Spy in the Coffee Machine* (Oneworld Publications, 2008).

K. D. Mitnick and W. L. Simon, *The Art of Deception* (Wiley, 2003).

C. P. Pfleeger and S. L. Pfleeger, *Security in Computing* (Prentice Hall, 2006).

F. Piper and S. Murphy, *Cryptography: A Very Short Introduction* (Oxford University Press, 2002).

B. Schneier, *Secrets and Lies* (Wiley, 2004).

B. Schneier, *Beyond Fear: Thinking Sensibly about Security in an Uncertain World* (Springer, 2003).

The disruptive computer

C. M. Christensen, *The Innovator's Dilemma: When New Technologies Cause Great Firms to Fail* (Harvard Business School Press, 1997).

C. M. Christenson and M. E. Raynor, *The Innovator's Solution: Creating and Sustaining Successful Growth* (Harvard Business School Press, 2003).

J. Gomez, *Print Is Dead* (Macmillan, 2007).

D. Silverman, *Typo: The Last American Typesetter or How I Made and Lost 4 Million Dollars* (Soft Skull Press, 2008).

The cloud computer

I. Ayres, *Super Crunchers* (John Murray, 2008).

N. G. Carr, *Does IT Matter? Information Technology and the Corrosion of Competitive Advantage* (Harvard Business School Press, 2004).

N. G. Carr, *The Big Switch: Rewiring the World, from 'Edison' to 'Google'* (W. W. Norton, 2009).

B. Mezrich, *The Accidental Billionaires: The Founding of Facebook – A Tale of Sex, Money, Genius and Betrayal* (Doubleday, 2010).
R. E. Stross, *Planet Google* (Atlantic Books, 2009).
B. Tancer, *Click* (Hyperion, 2009).
D. Tapscott and A. D. Williams, *Wikinomics* (Atlantic Books, 2006).

The next computer

N. G. Carr, *The Big Switch: Rewiring the World, from 'Edison' to 'Google'* (W. W. Norton, 2009).
J. Gleick, *The Information: A History, a Theory, a Flood* (Fourth Estate, 2011).
T. Wu, *The Master Switch* (Atlantic Books, 2011).
J. Zittrain, *The Future of the Internet: And How to Stop It* (Penguin Books, 2009).

Index

A

B

C

D

E

F

N

O

P

Q

R

S

T

U

V

W

X

Y

Z

STATISTICS

A Very Short Introduction

David J. Hand

Modern statistics is very different from the dry and dusty discipline of the popular imagination. In its place is an exciting subject which uses deep theory and powerful software tools to shed light and enable understanding. And it sheds this light on all aspects of our lives, enabling astronomers to explore the origins of the universe, archaeologists to investigate ancient civilisations, governments to understand how to benefit and improve society, and businesses to learn how best to provide goods and services. Aimed at readers with no prior mathematical knowledge, this *Very Short Introduction* explores and explains how statistics work, and how we can decipher them.

www.oup.com/vsi

ONLINE CATALOGUE

A Very Short Introduction

Our online catalogue is designed to make it easy to find your ideal Very Short Introduction. View the entire collection by subject area, watch author videos, read sample chapters, and download reading guides.

http://fds.oup.com/www.oup.co.uk/general/vsi/index.html